BABY NAME:

MW00885423

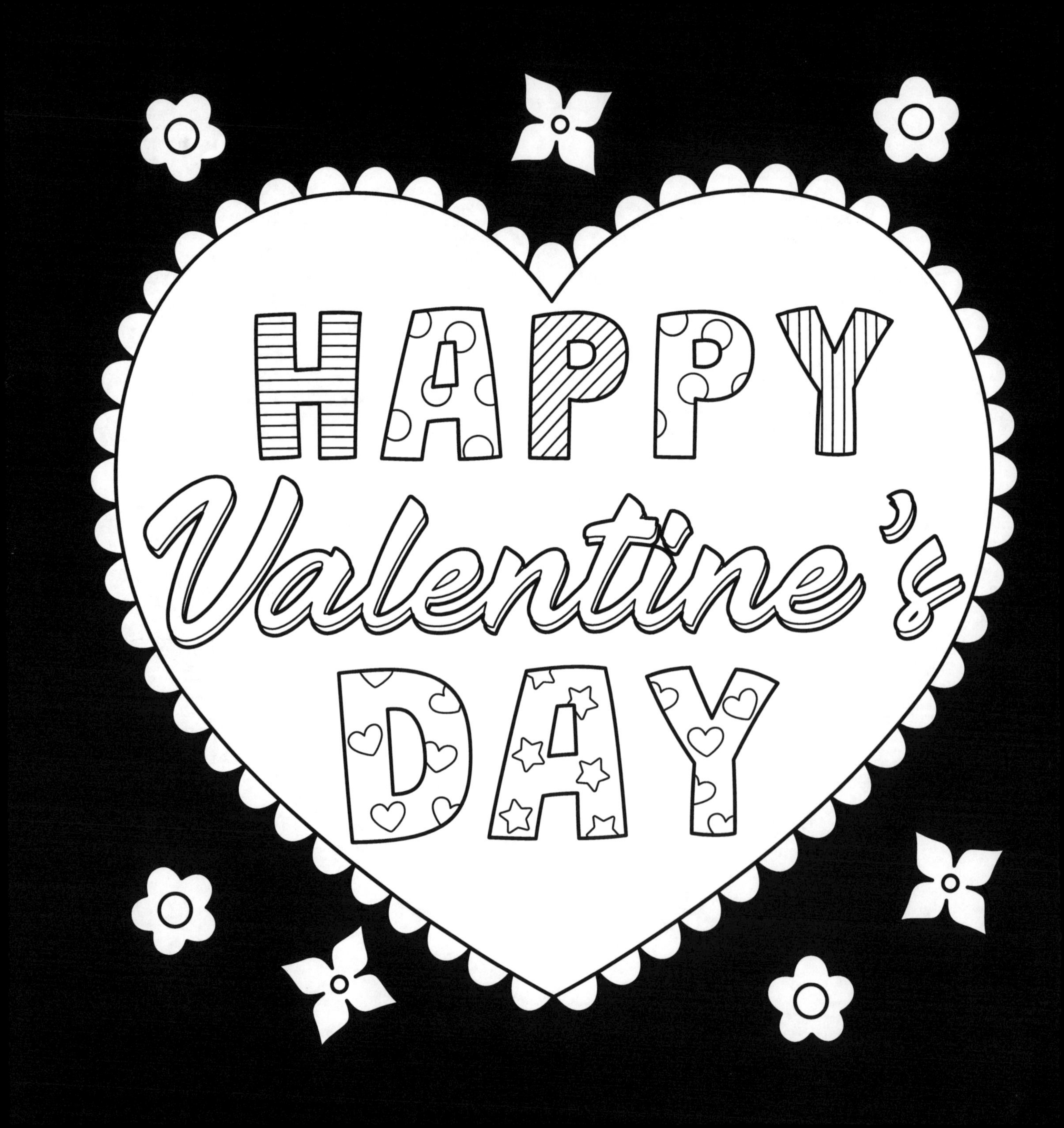
HAPPY
Happy Valentine's
DAY

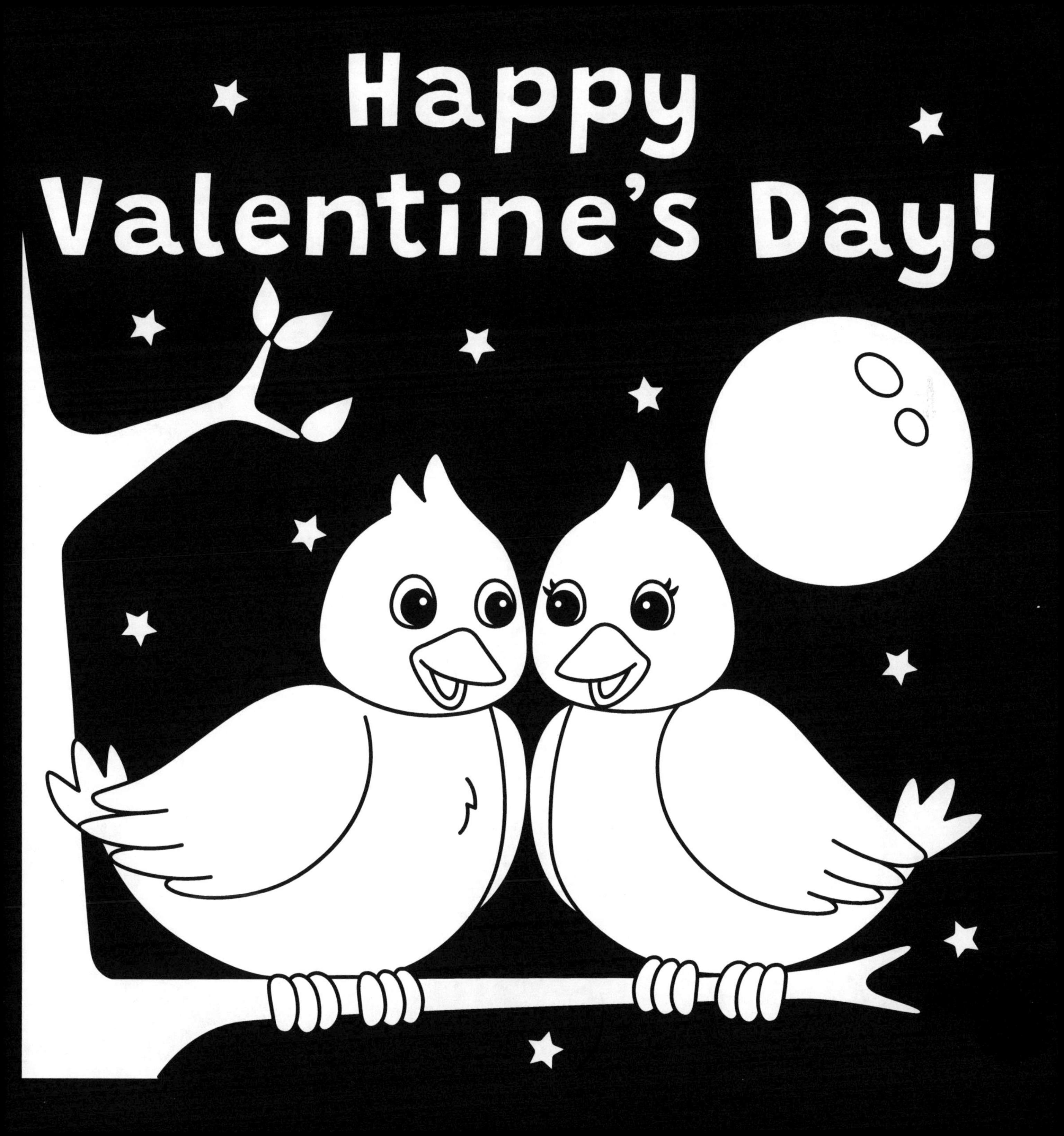
Happy
Valentine's Day!

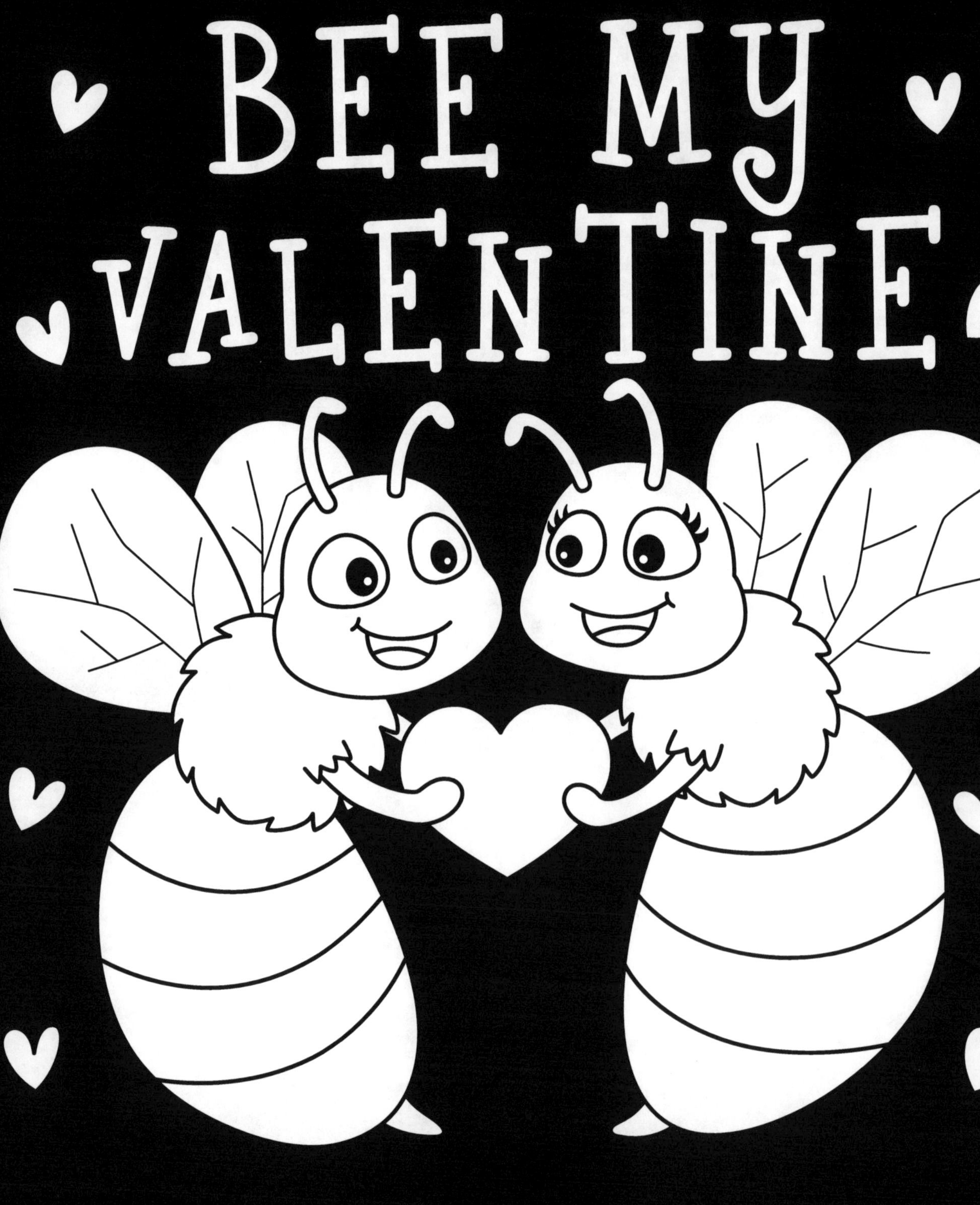
BEE MY
VALENTINE

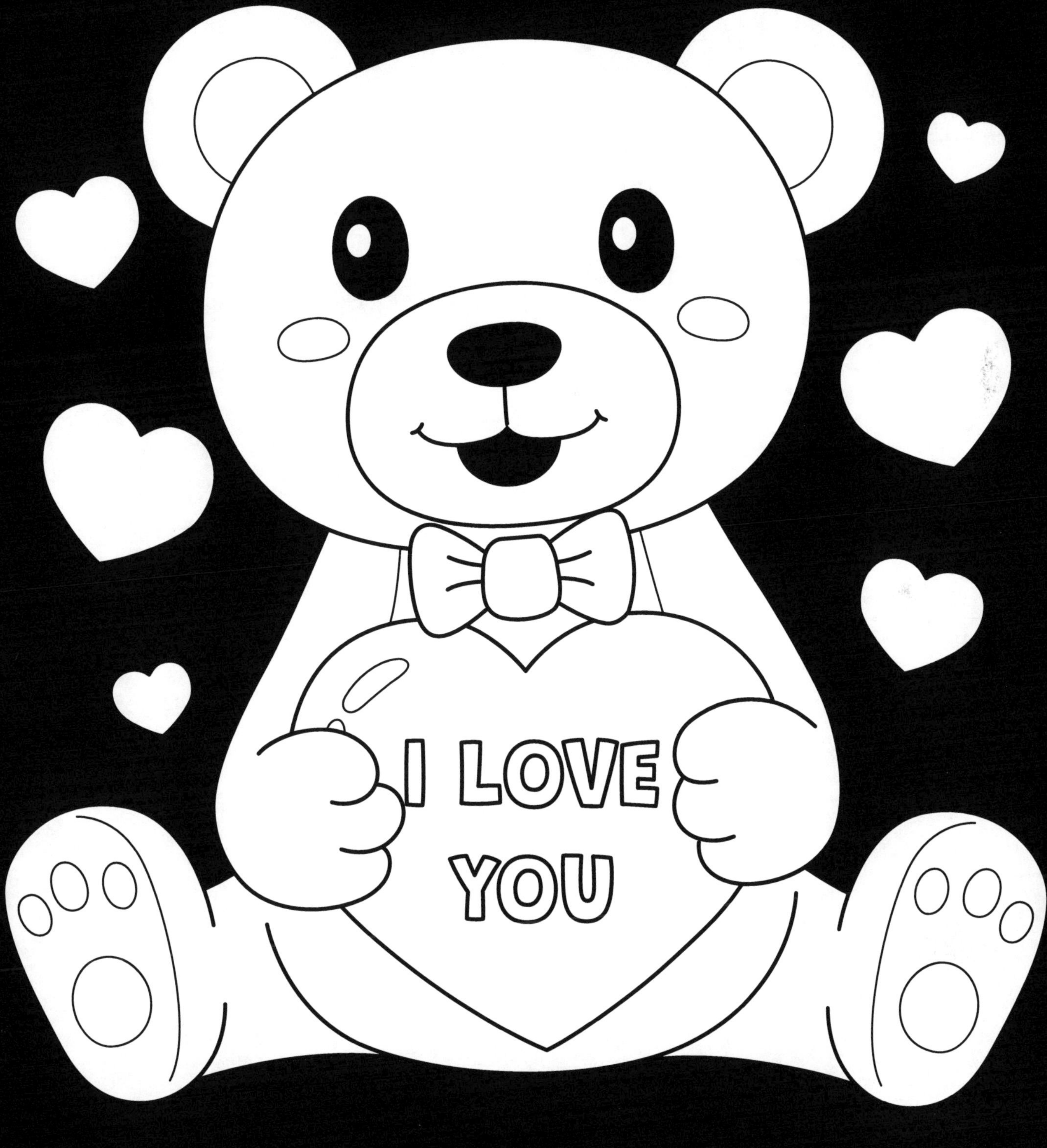
I LOVE
YOU

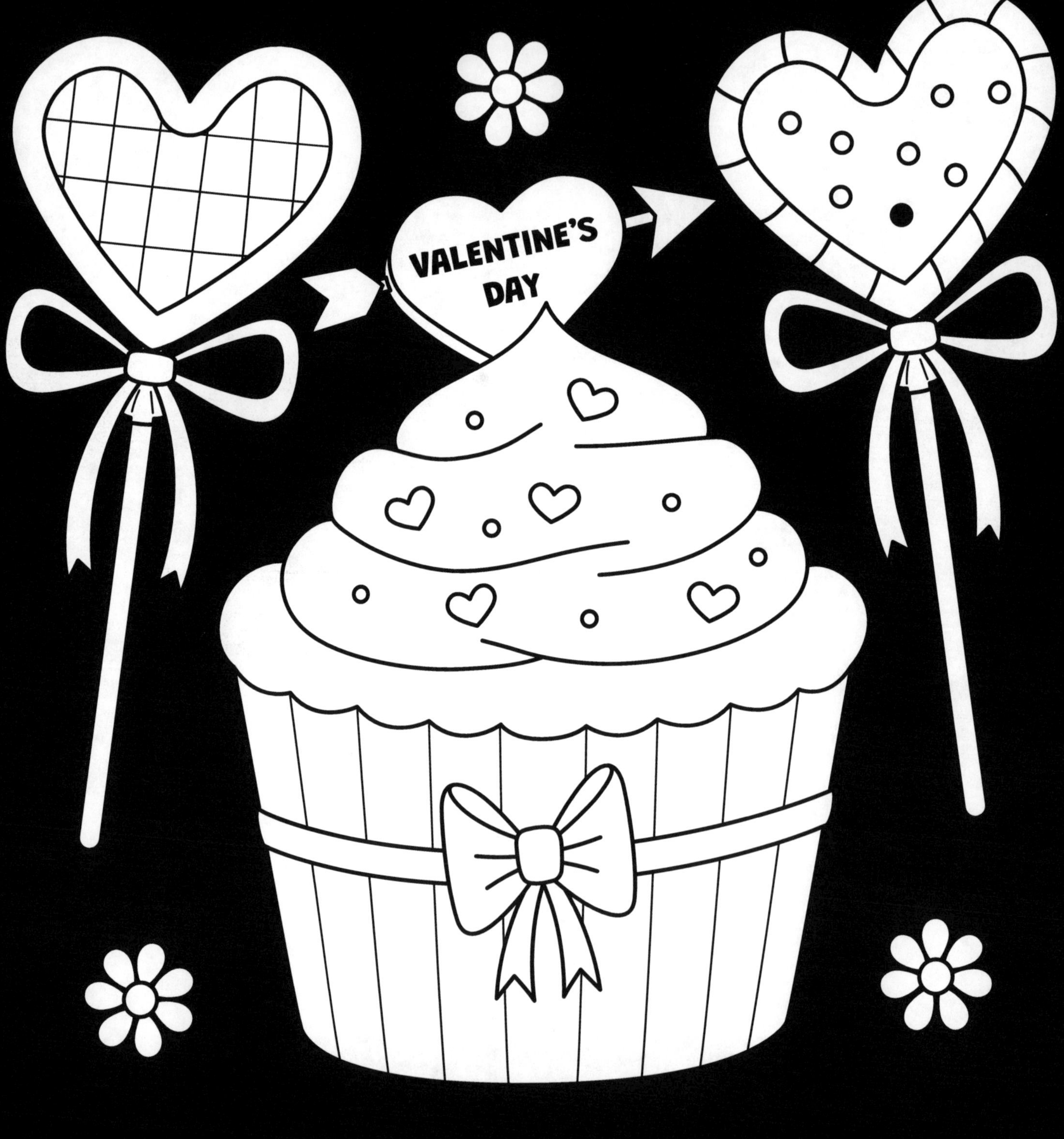
VALENTINE'S
DAY

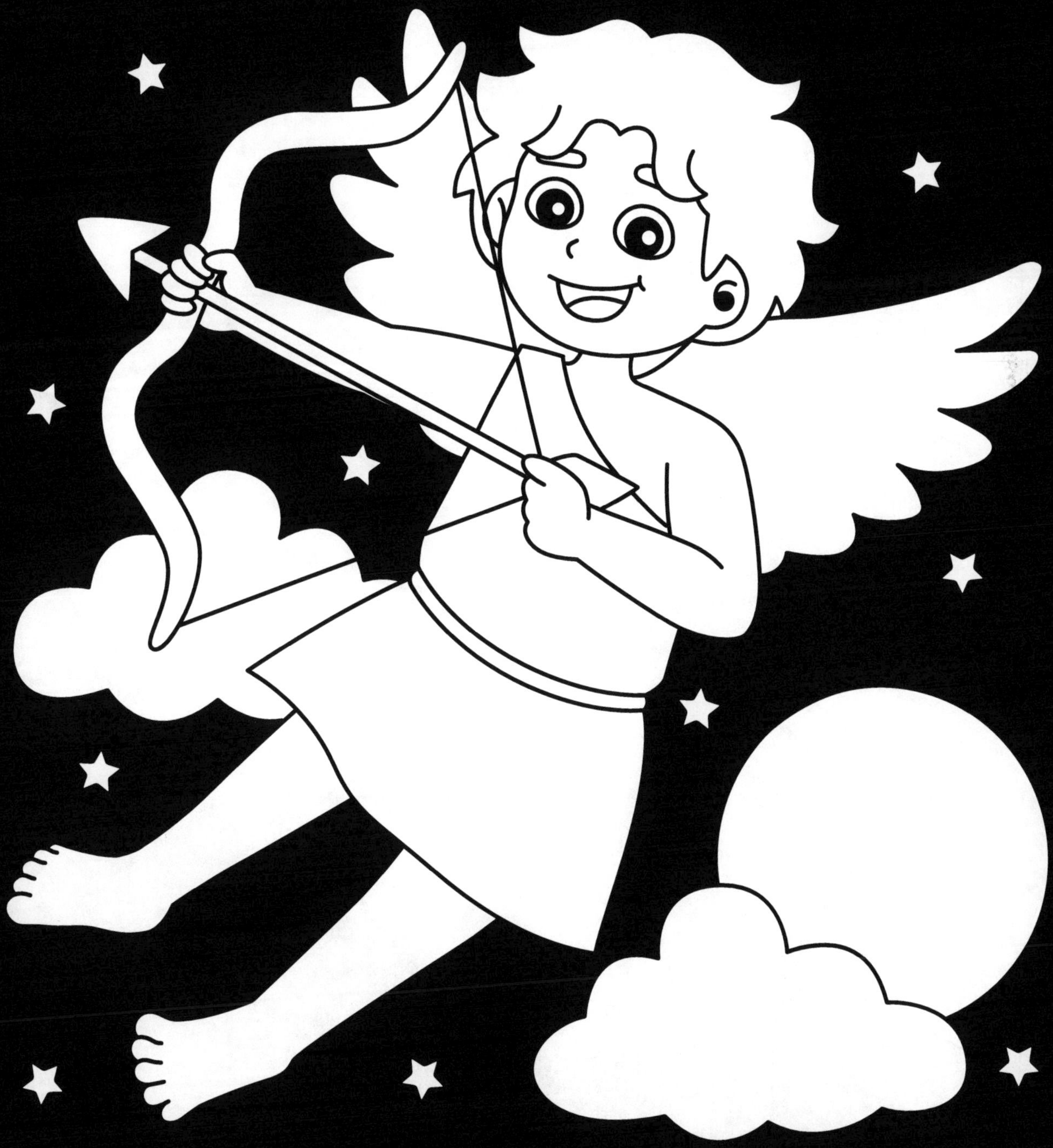

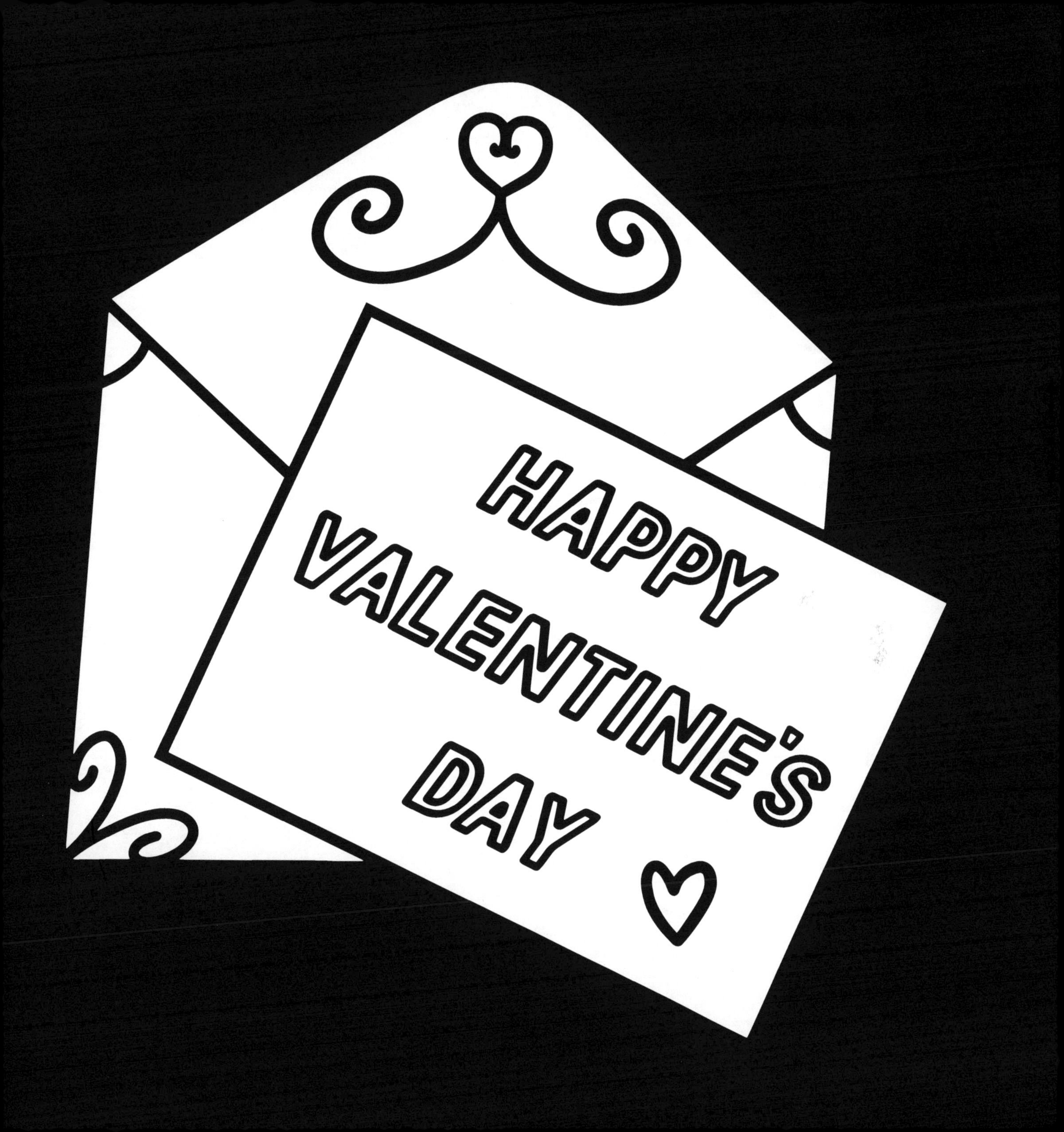
HAPPY
VALENTINE'S
DAY

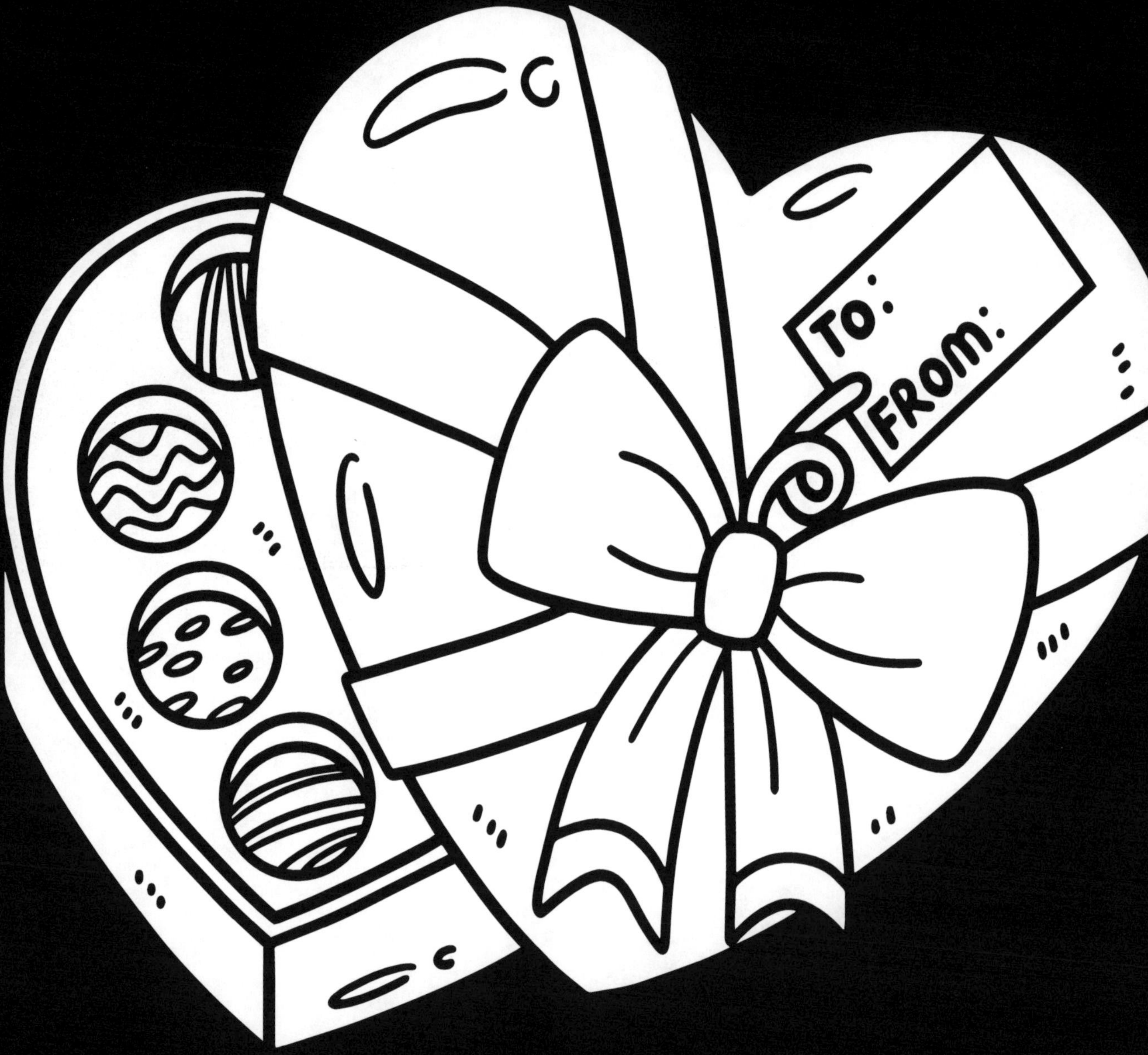
To:
FROM:

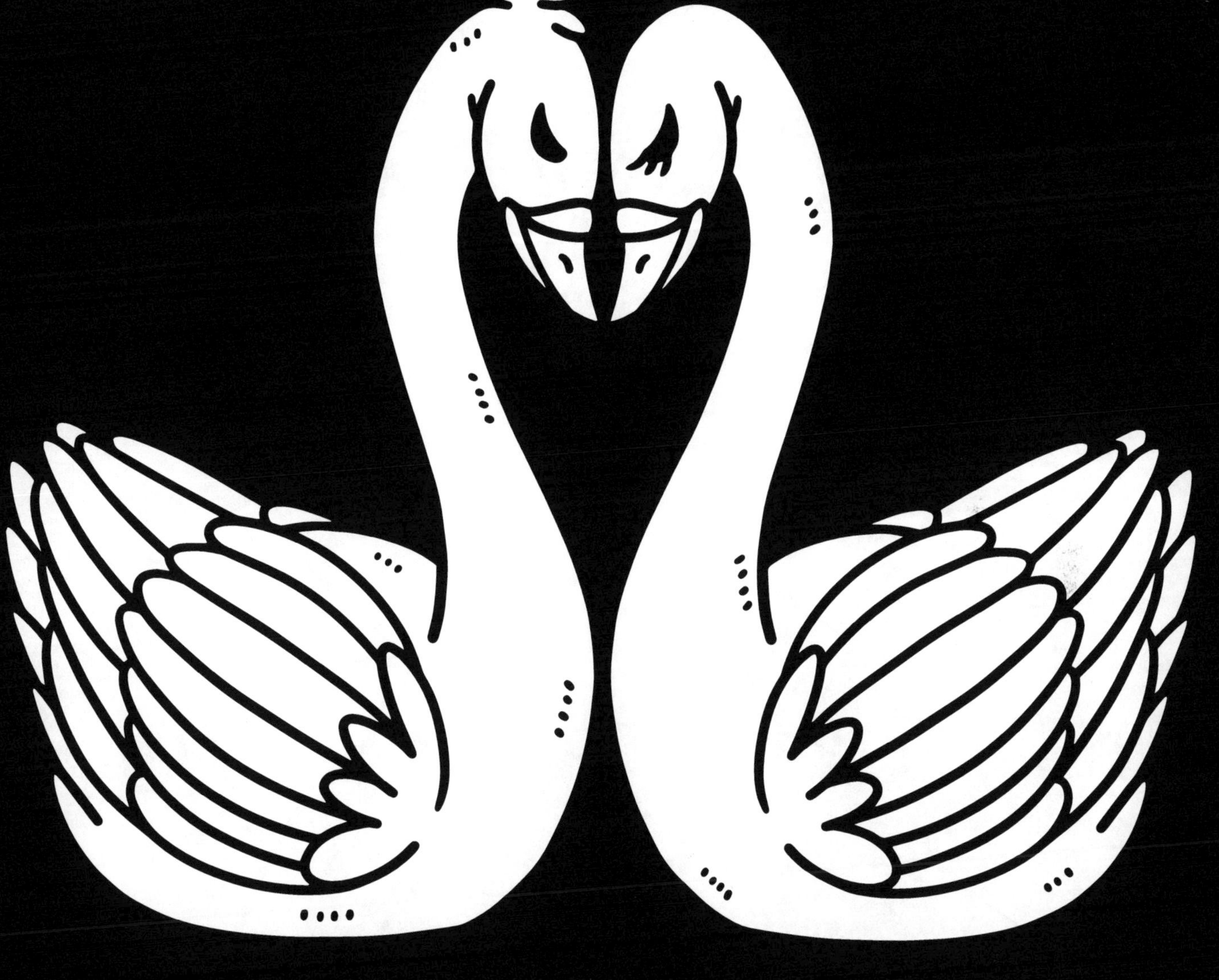

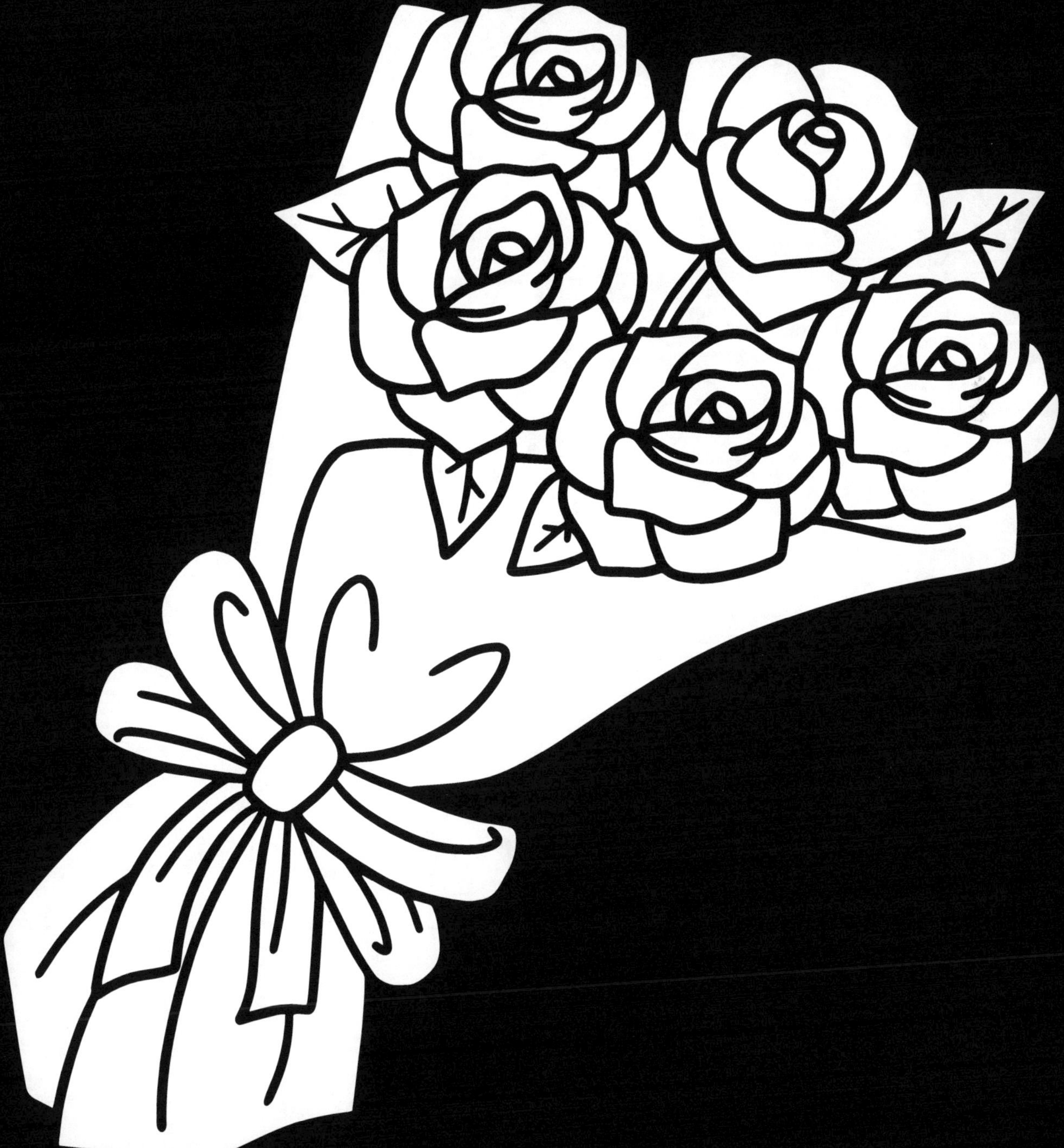

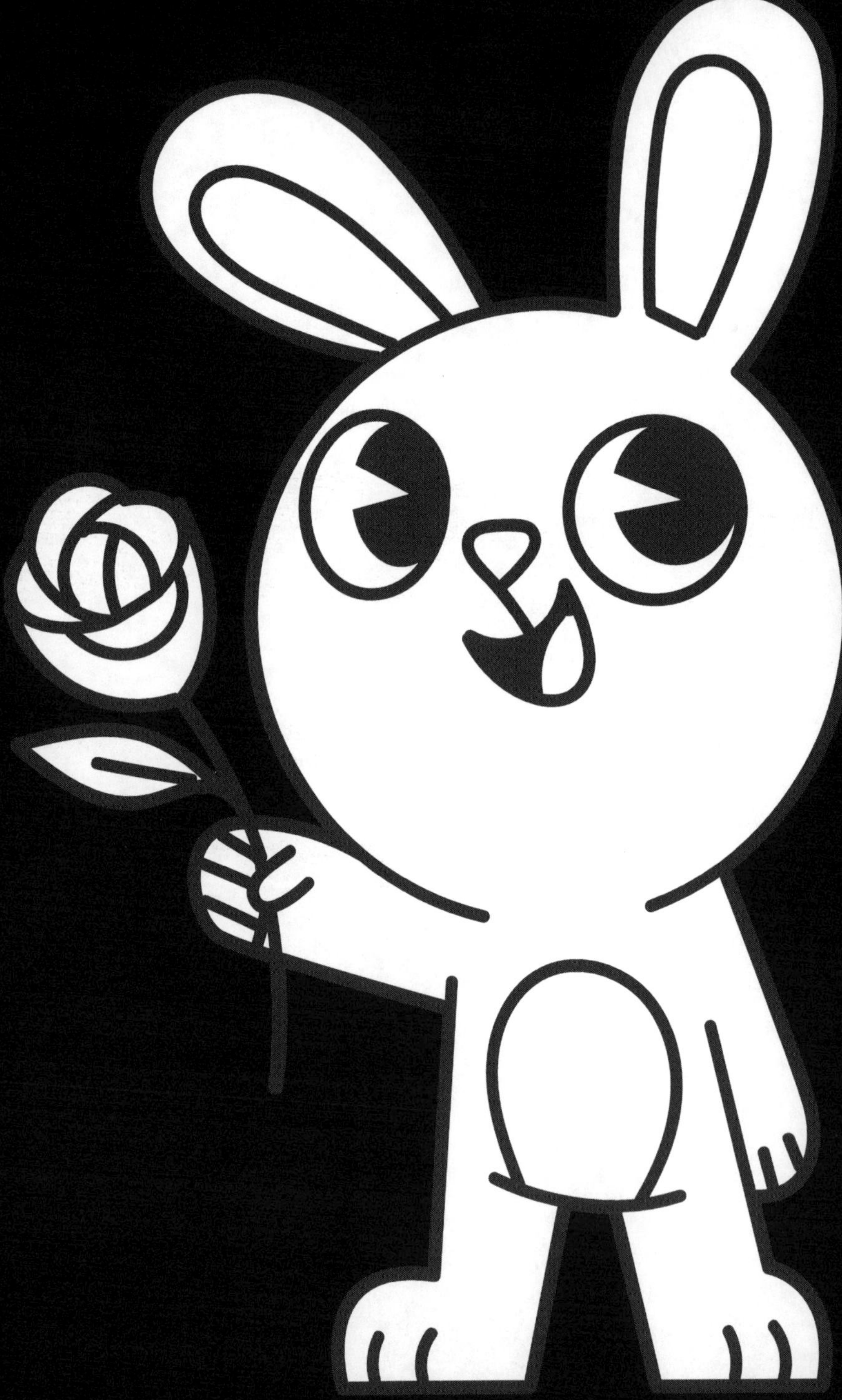

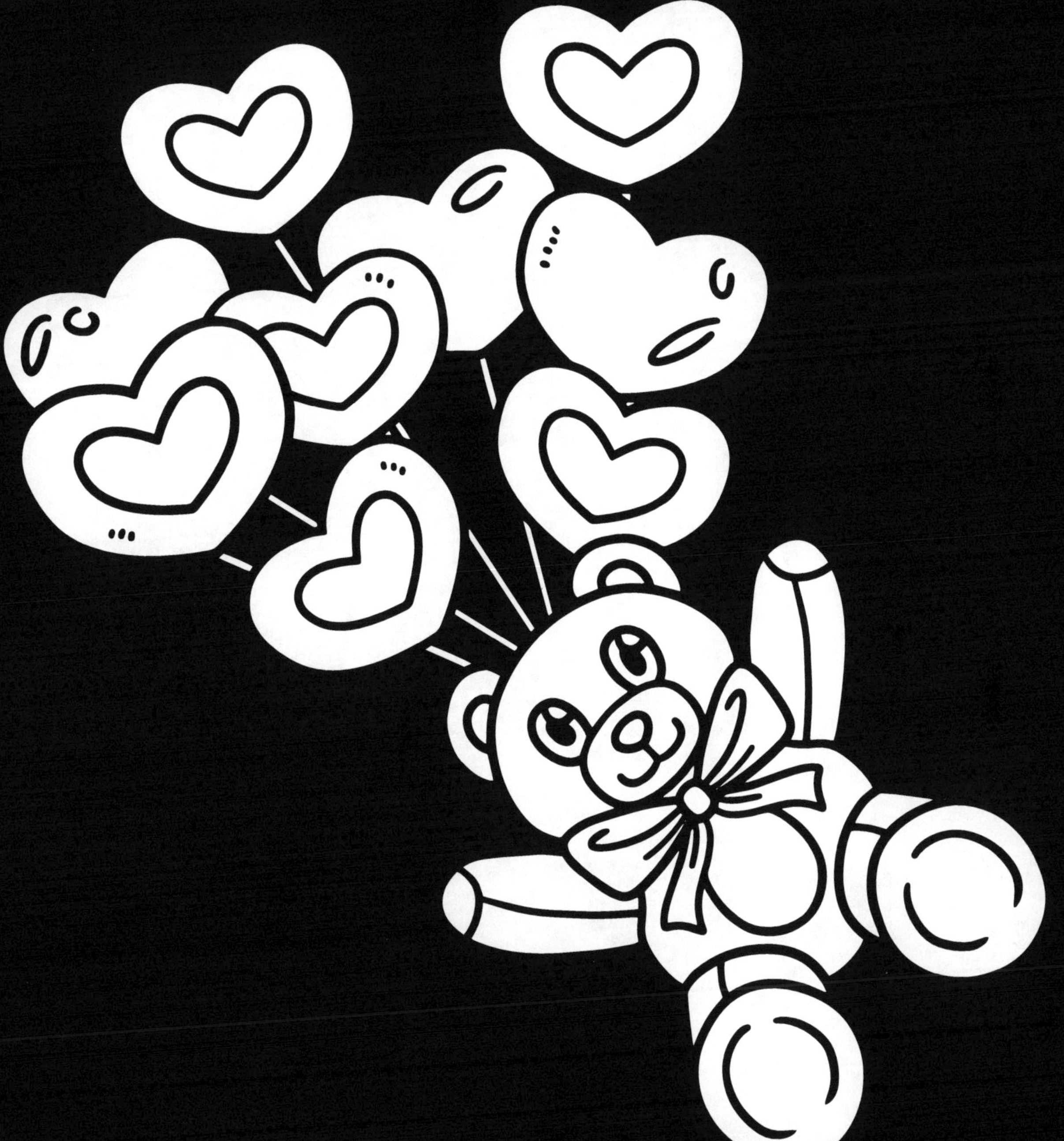

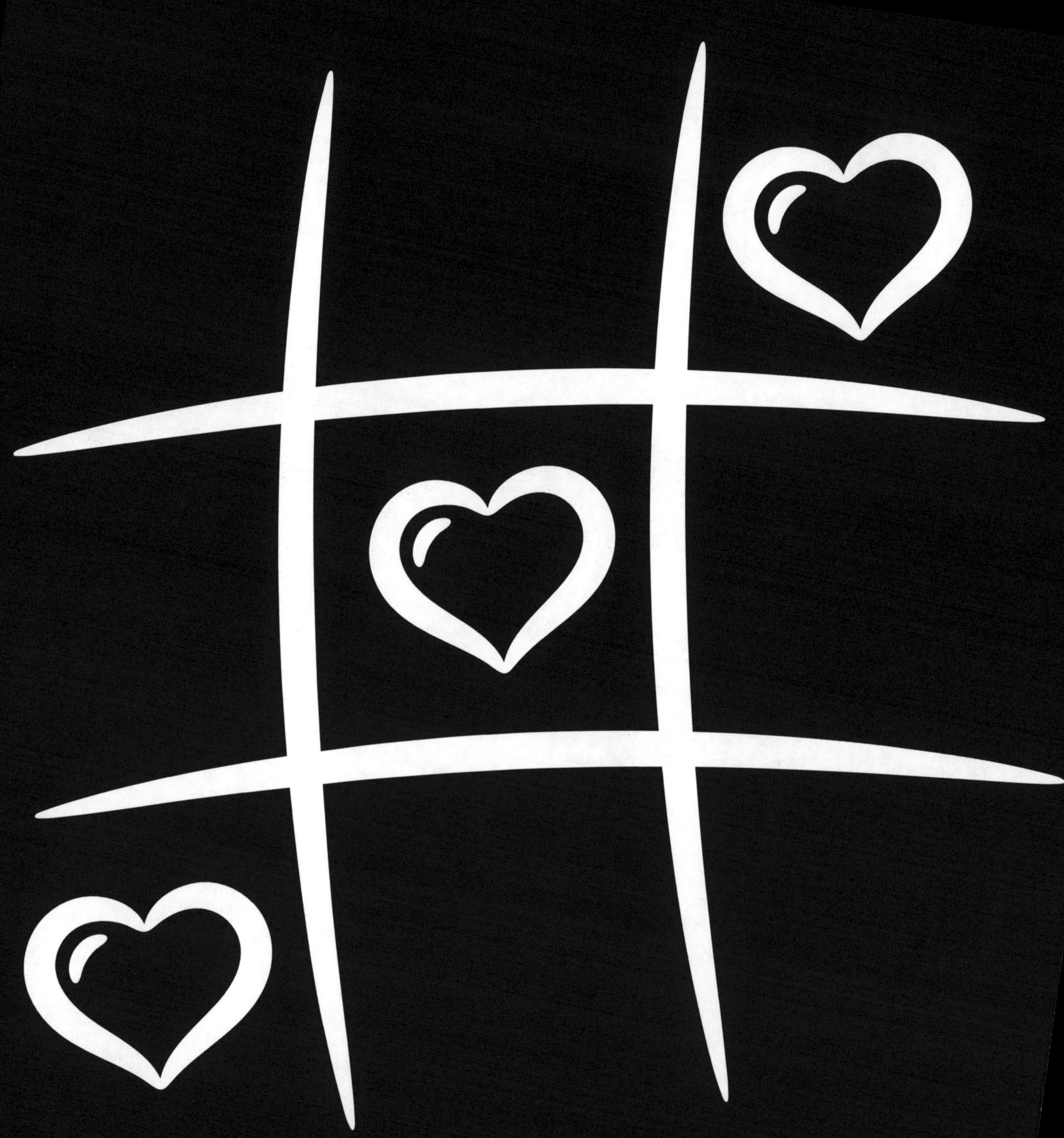

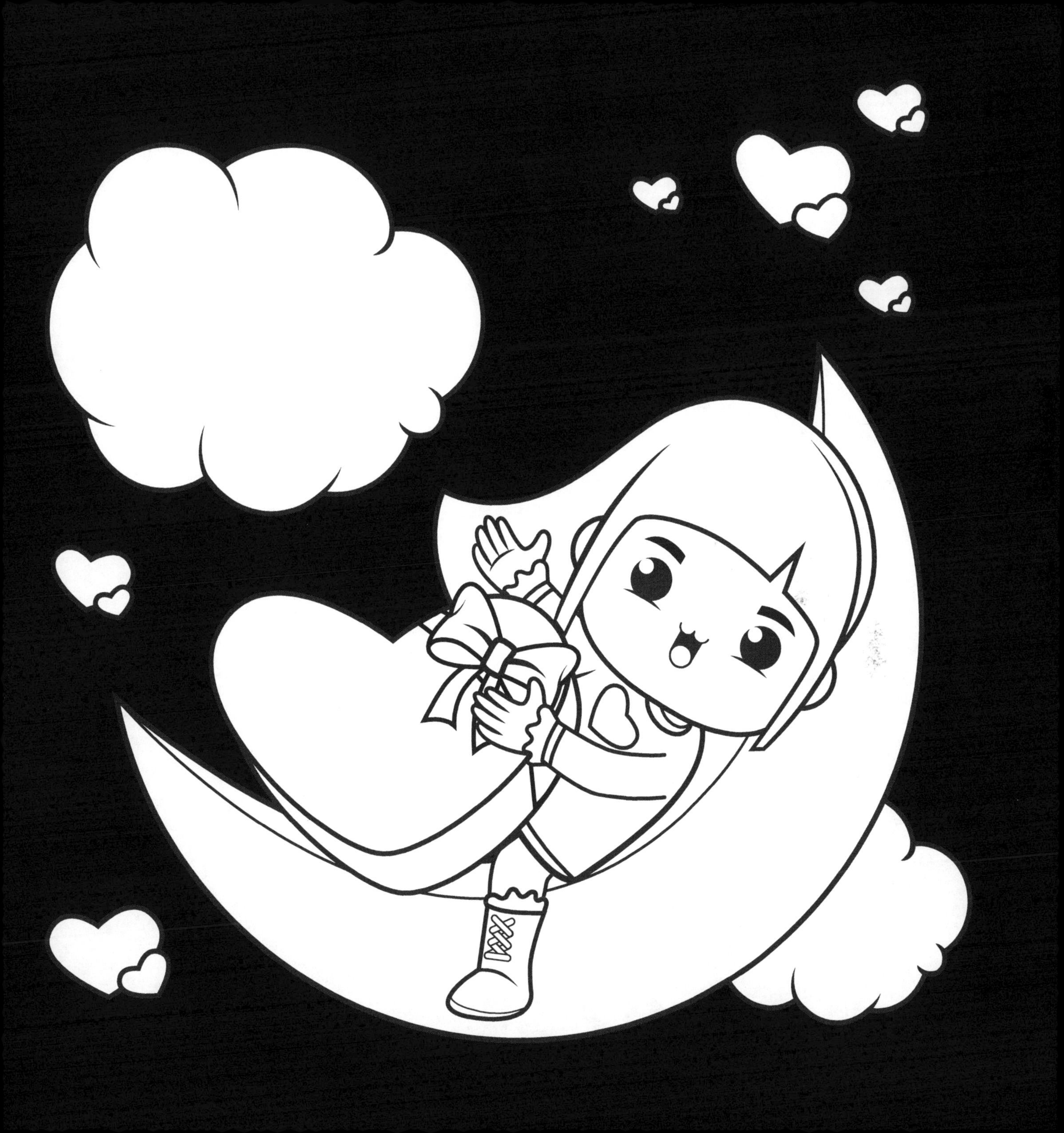

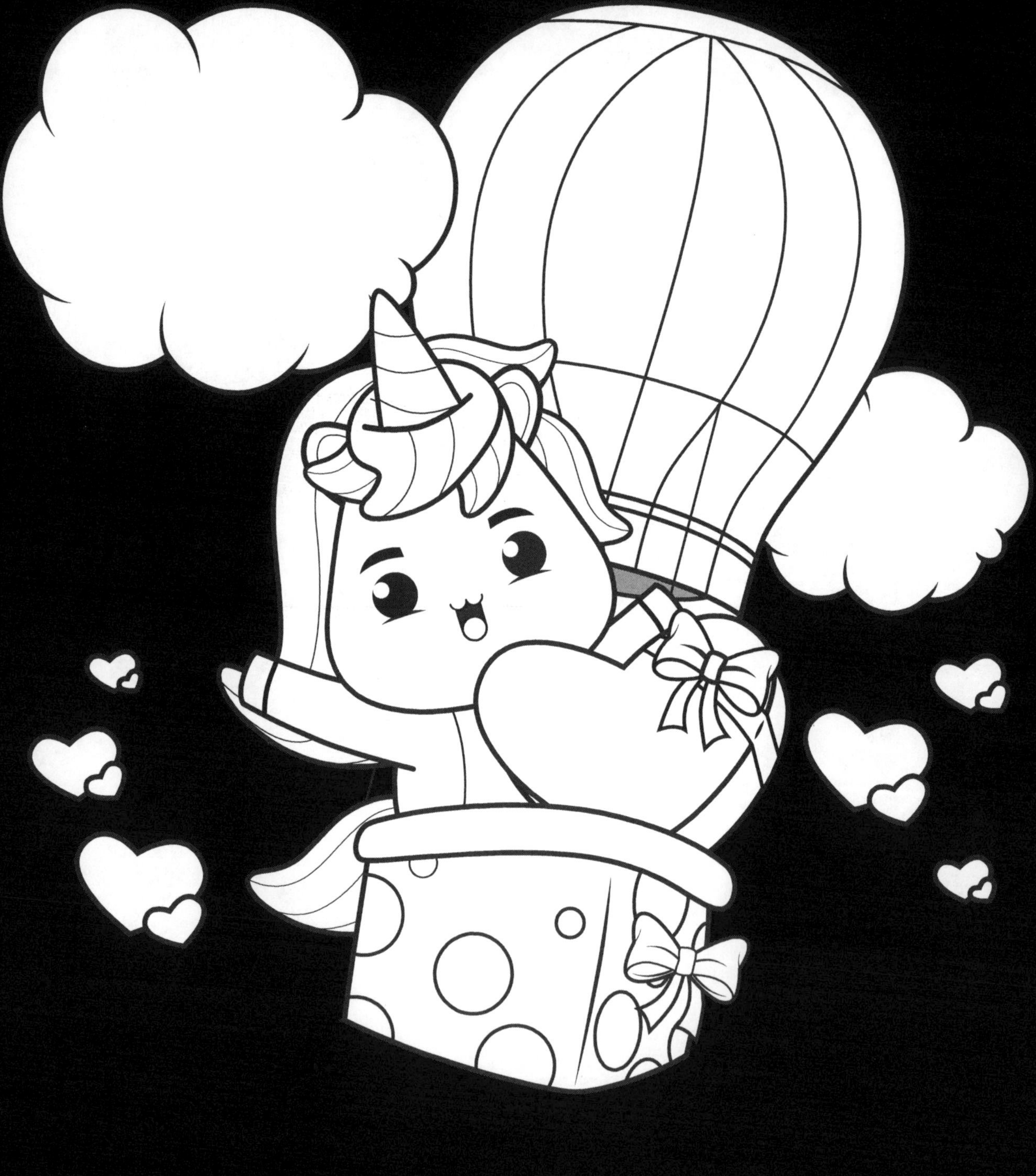

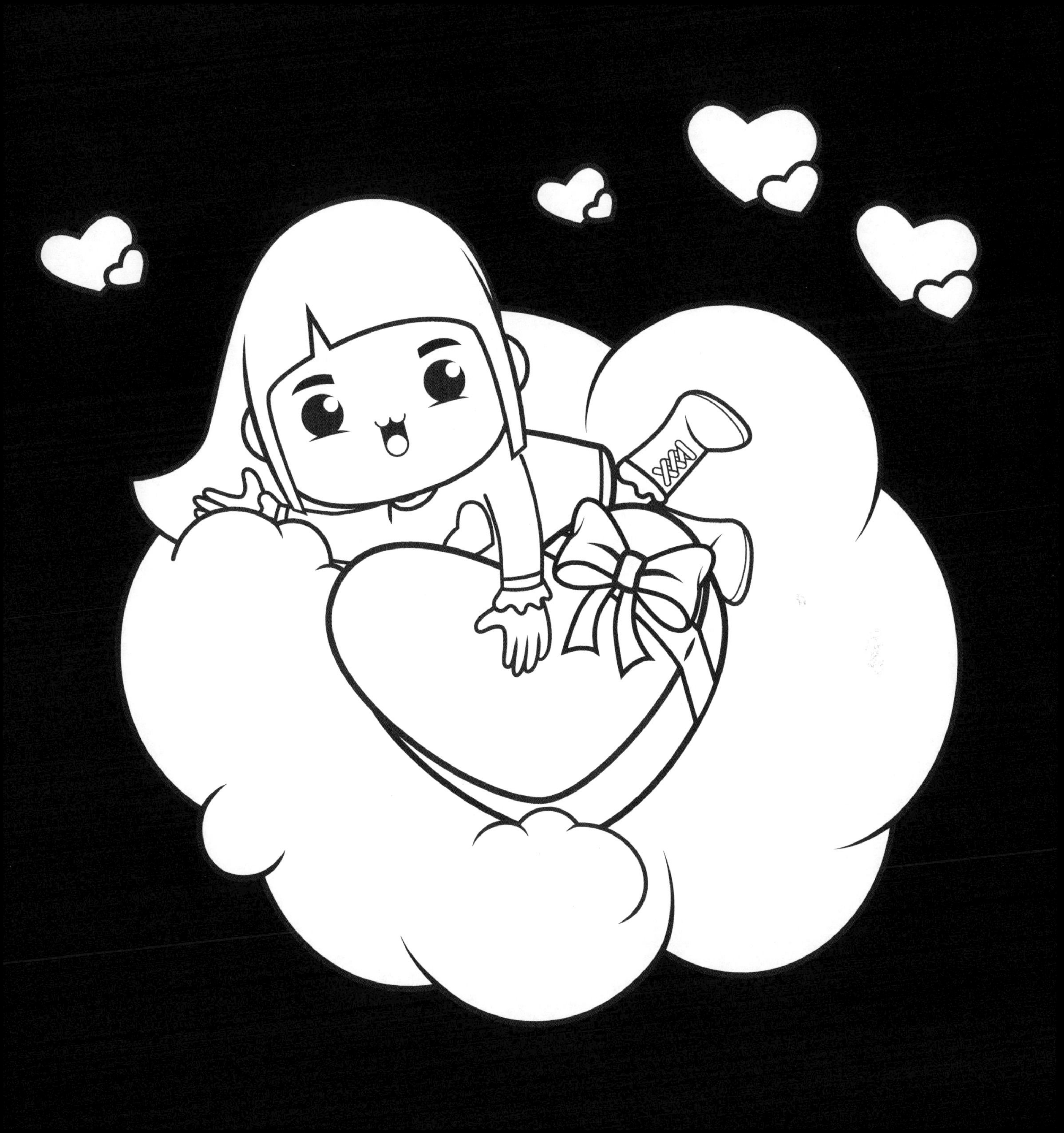

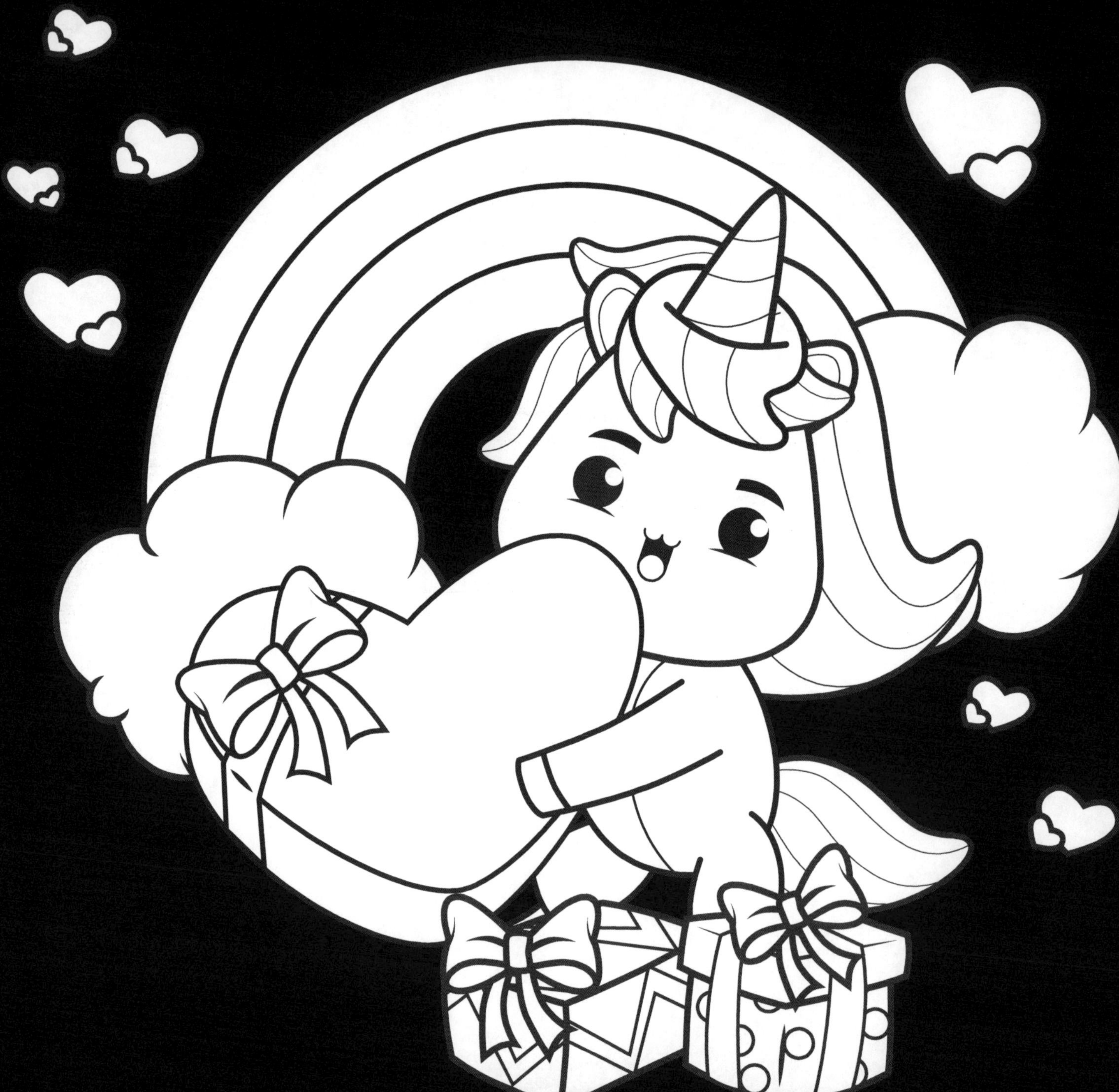

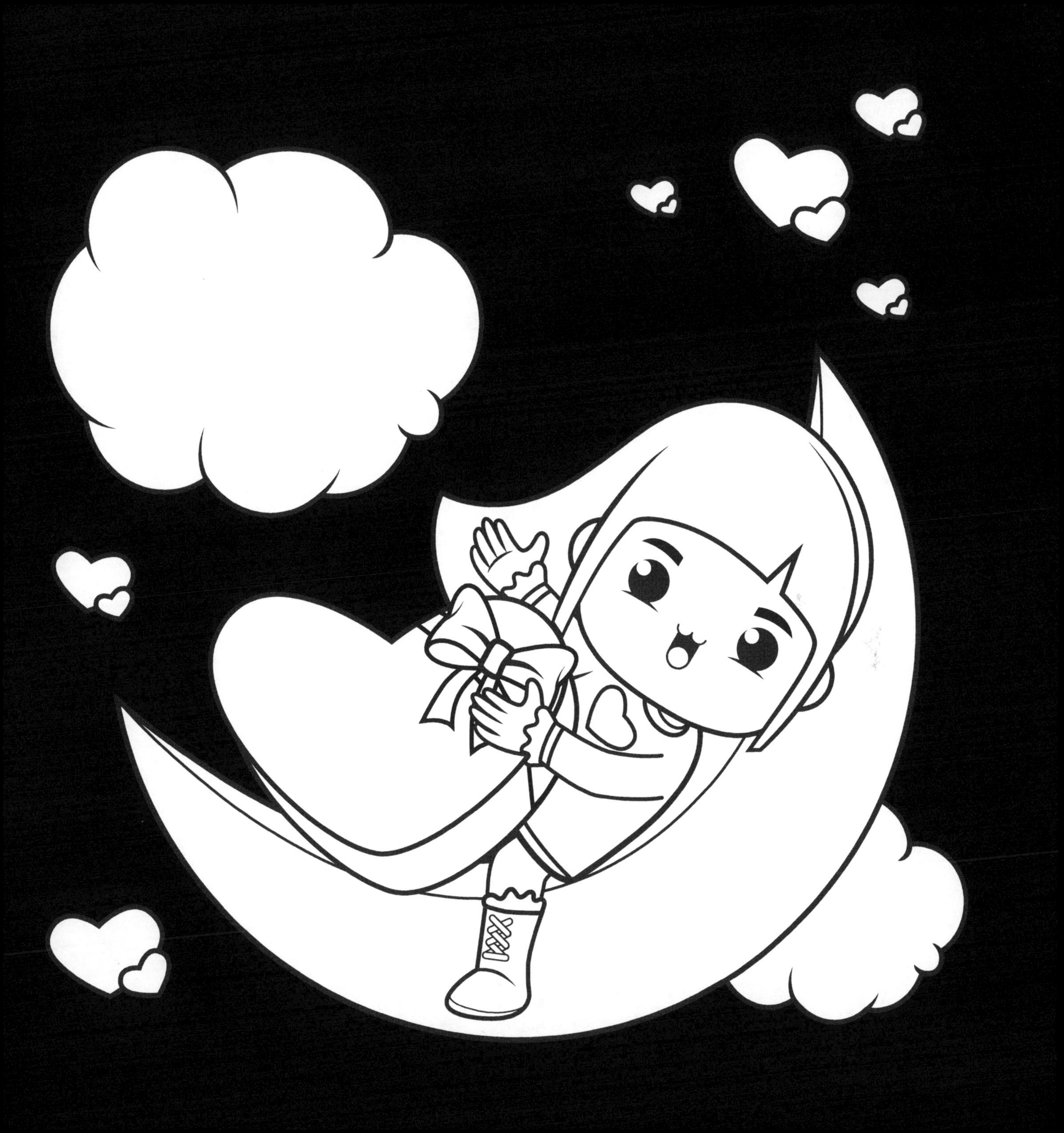

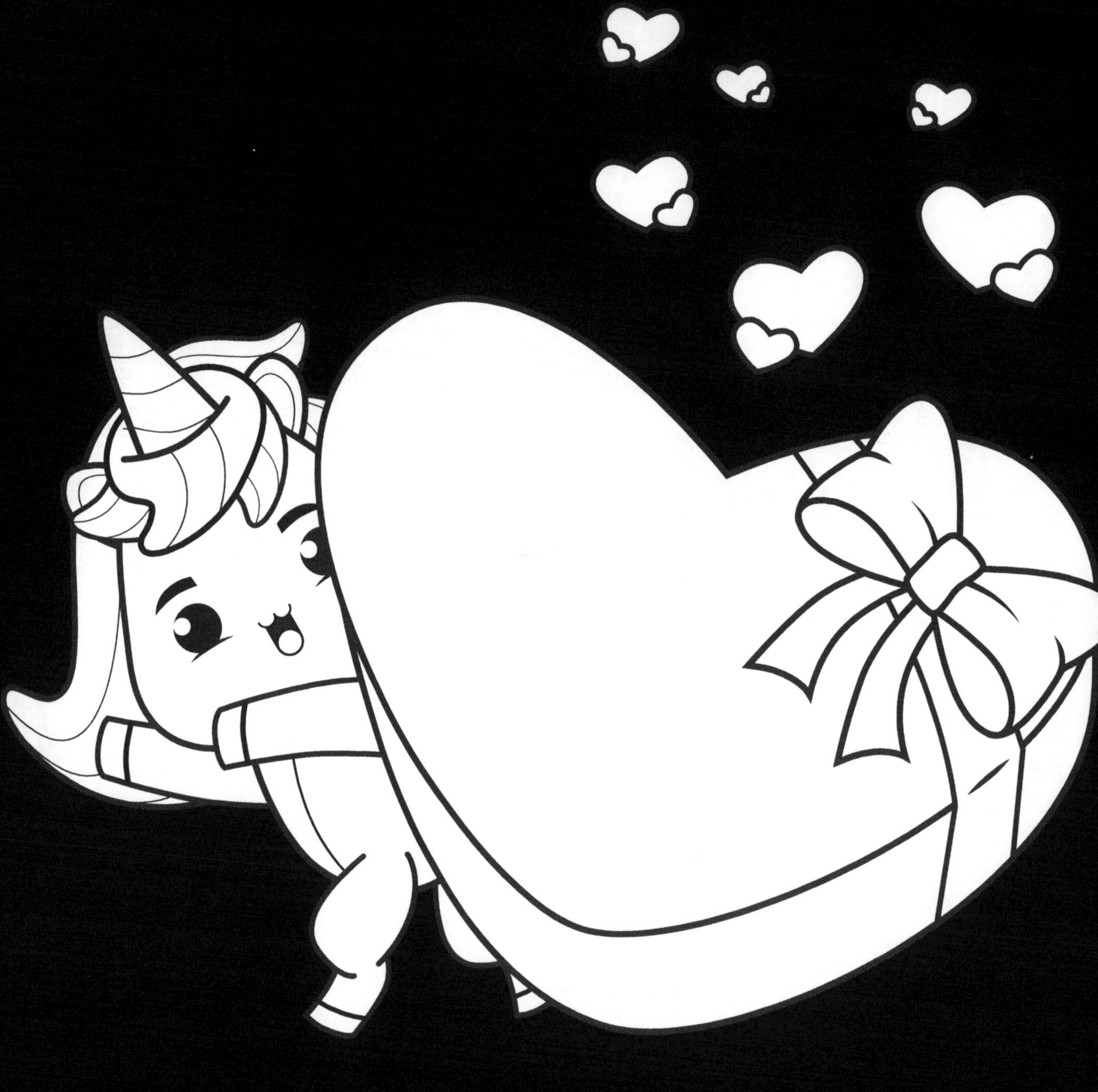

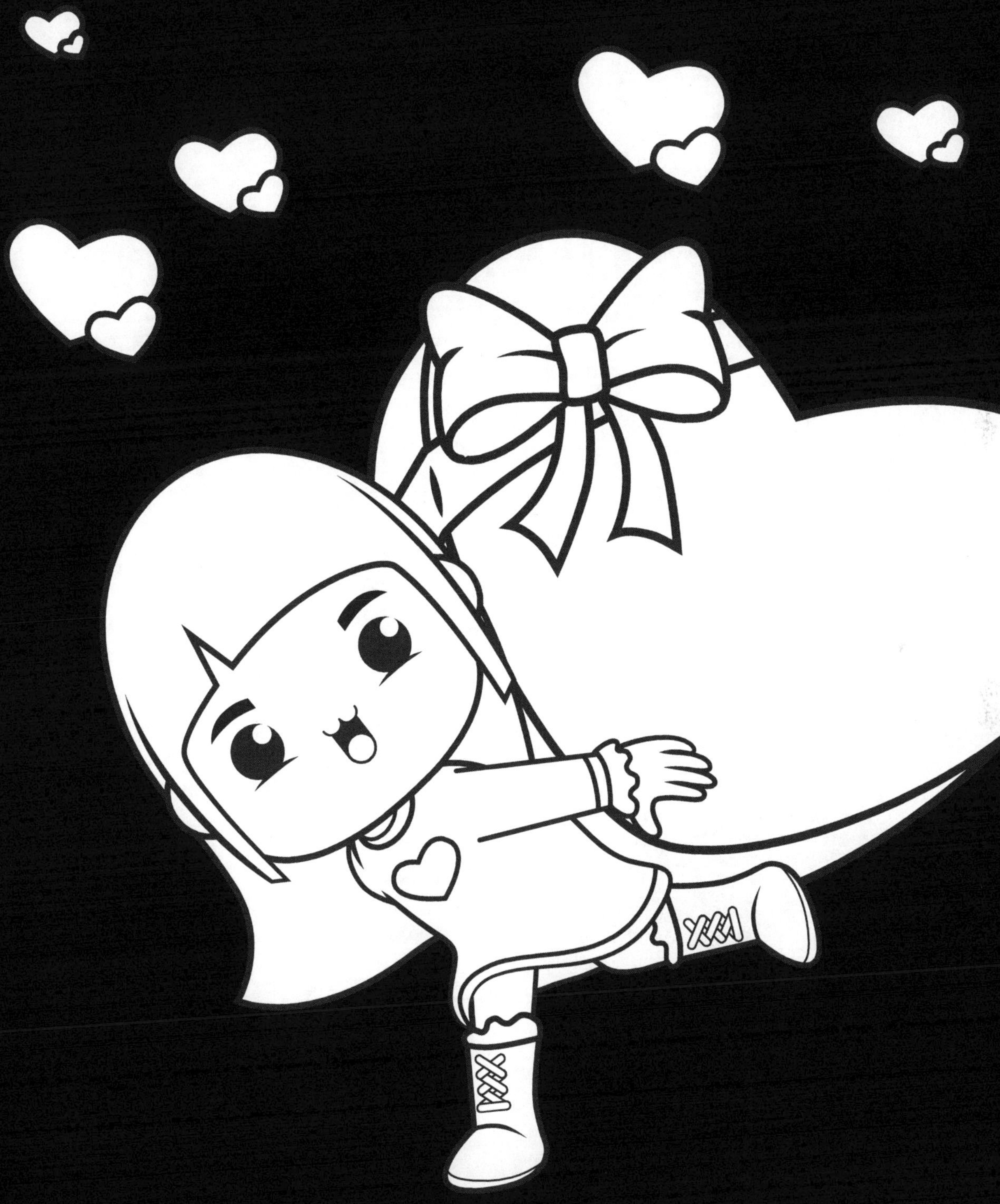

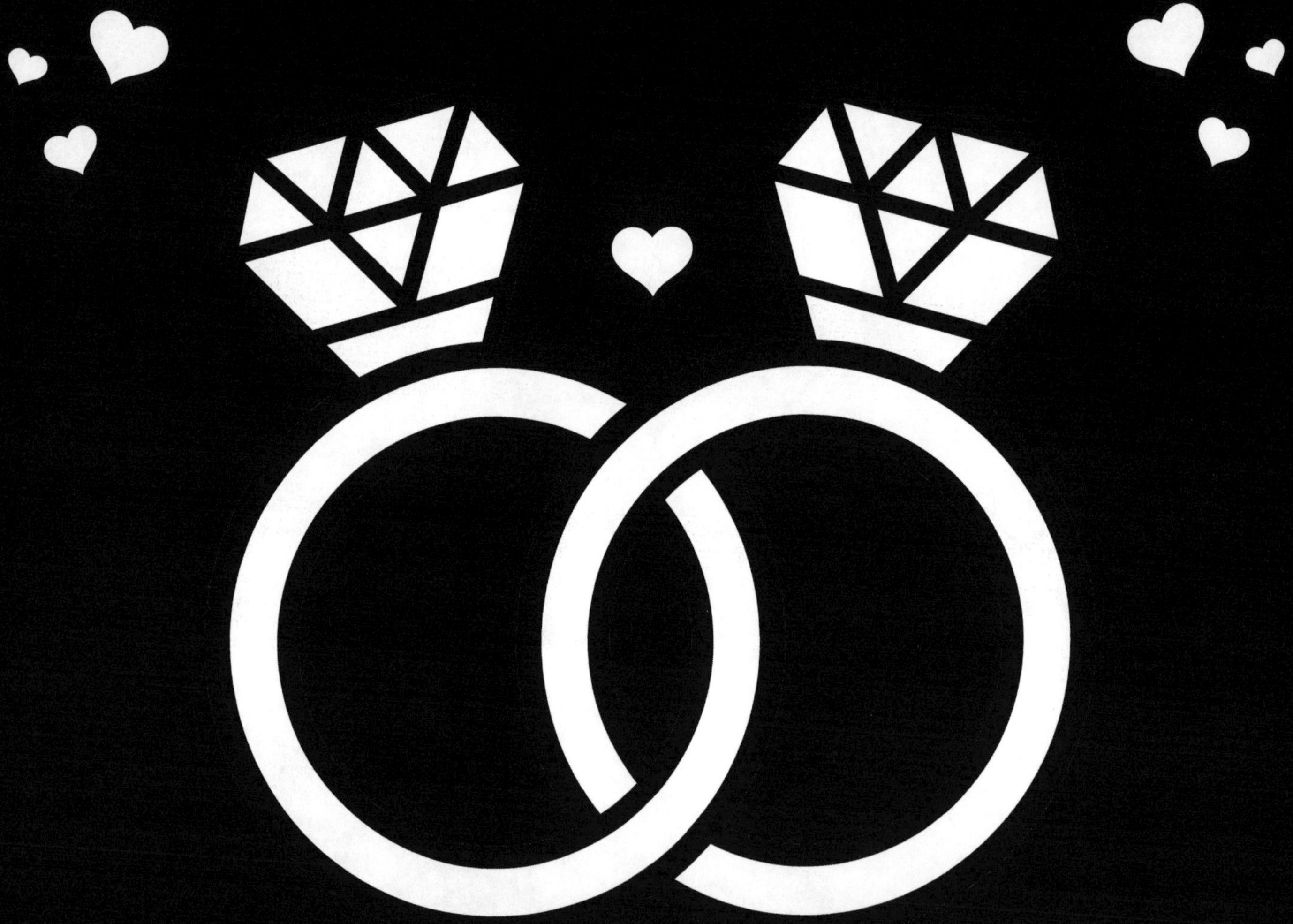

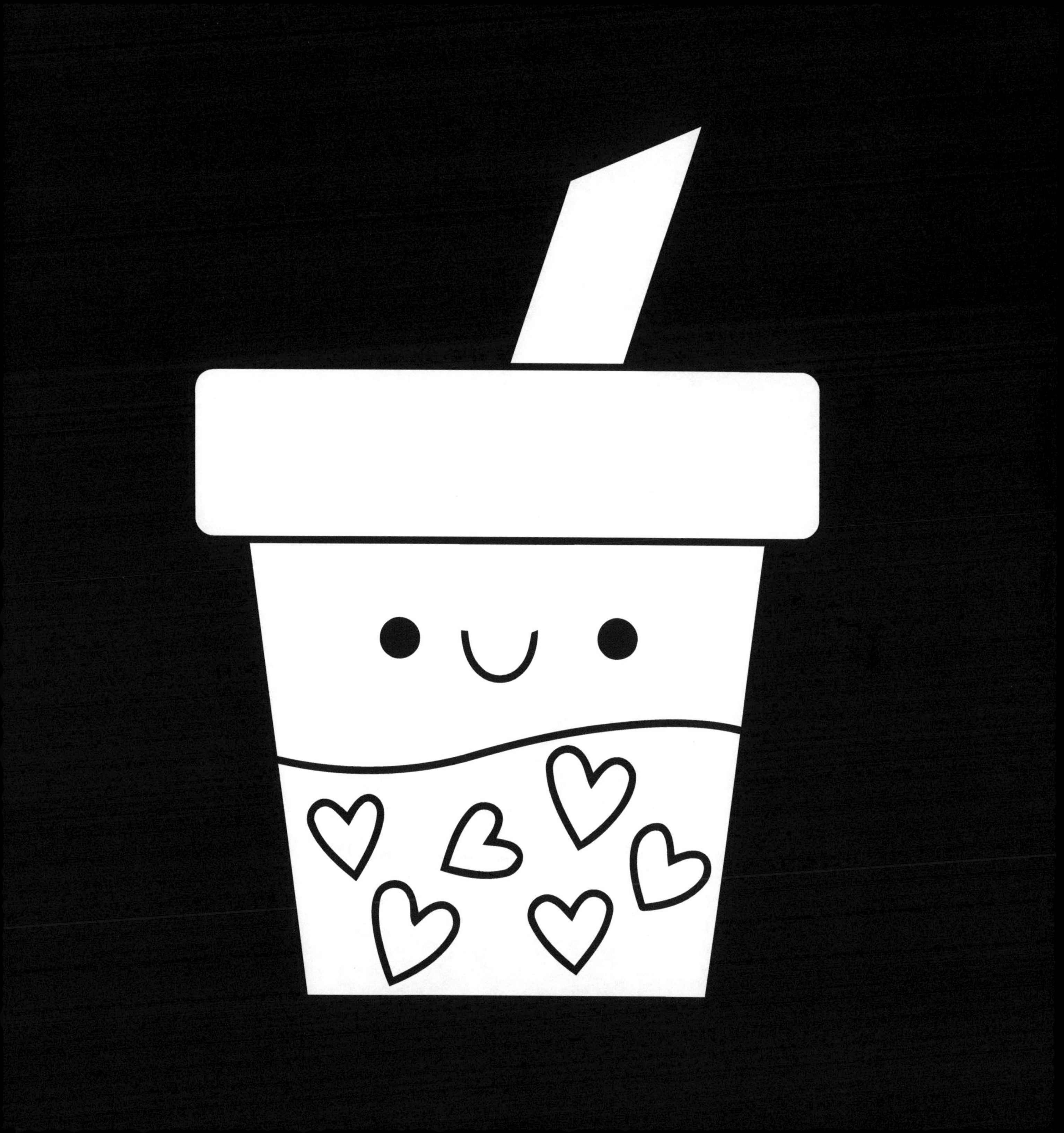

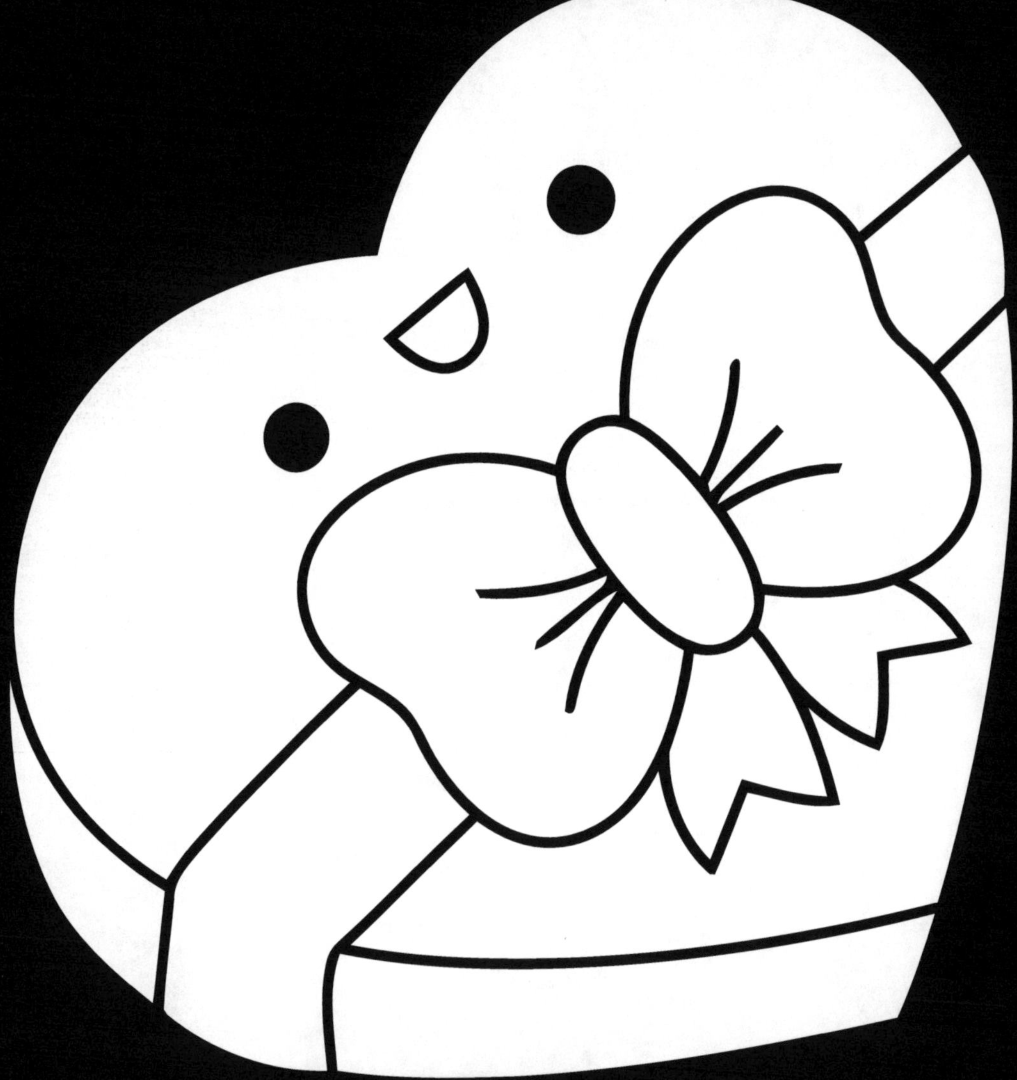

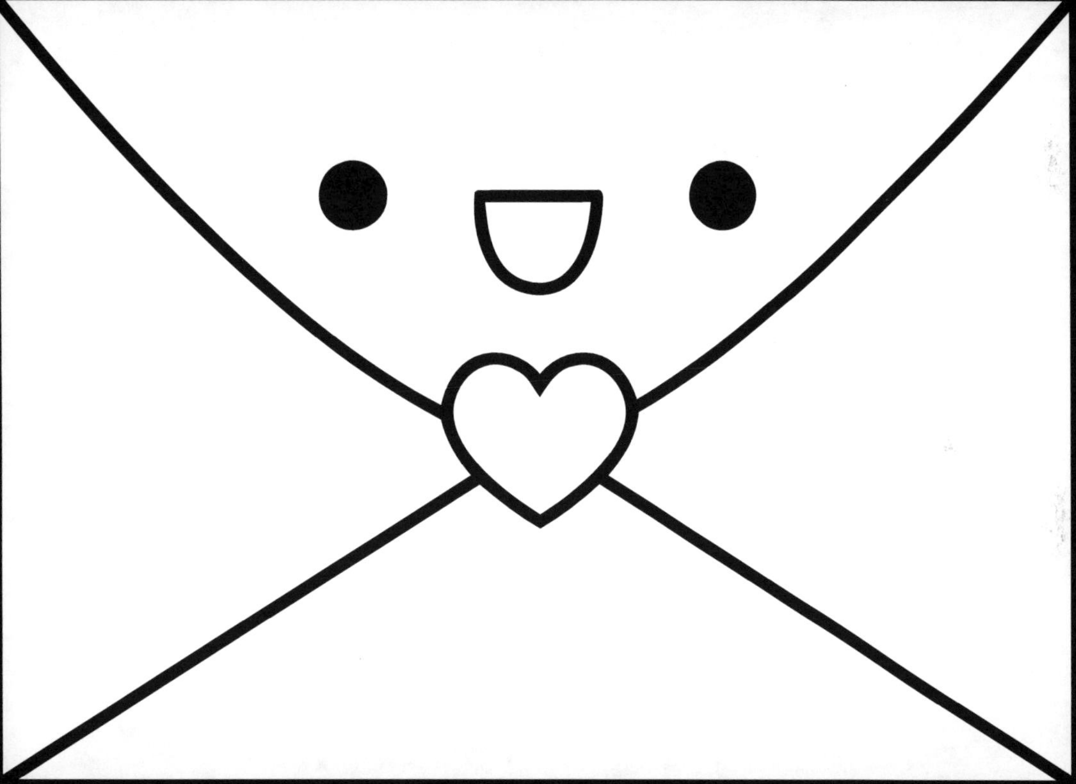

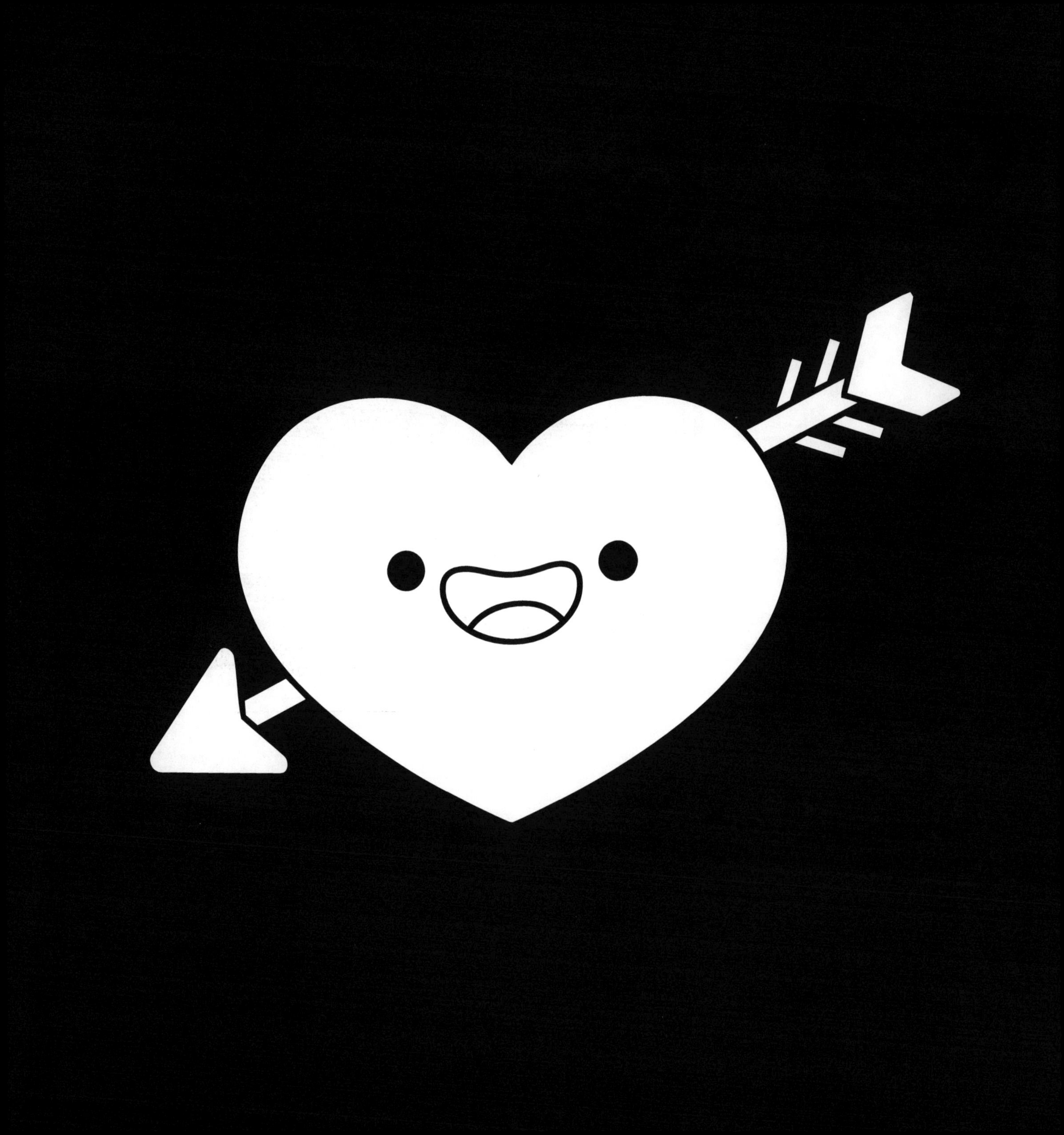

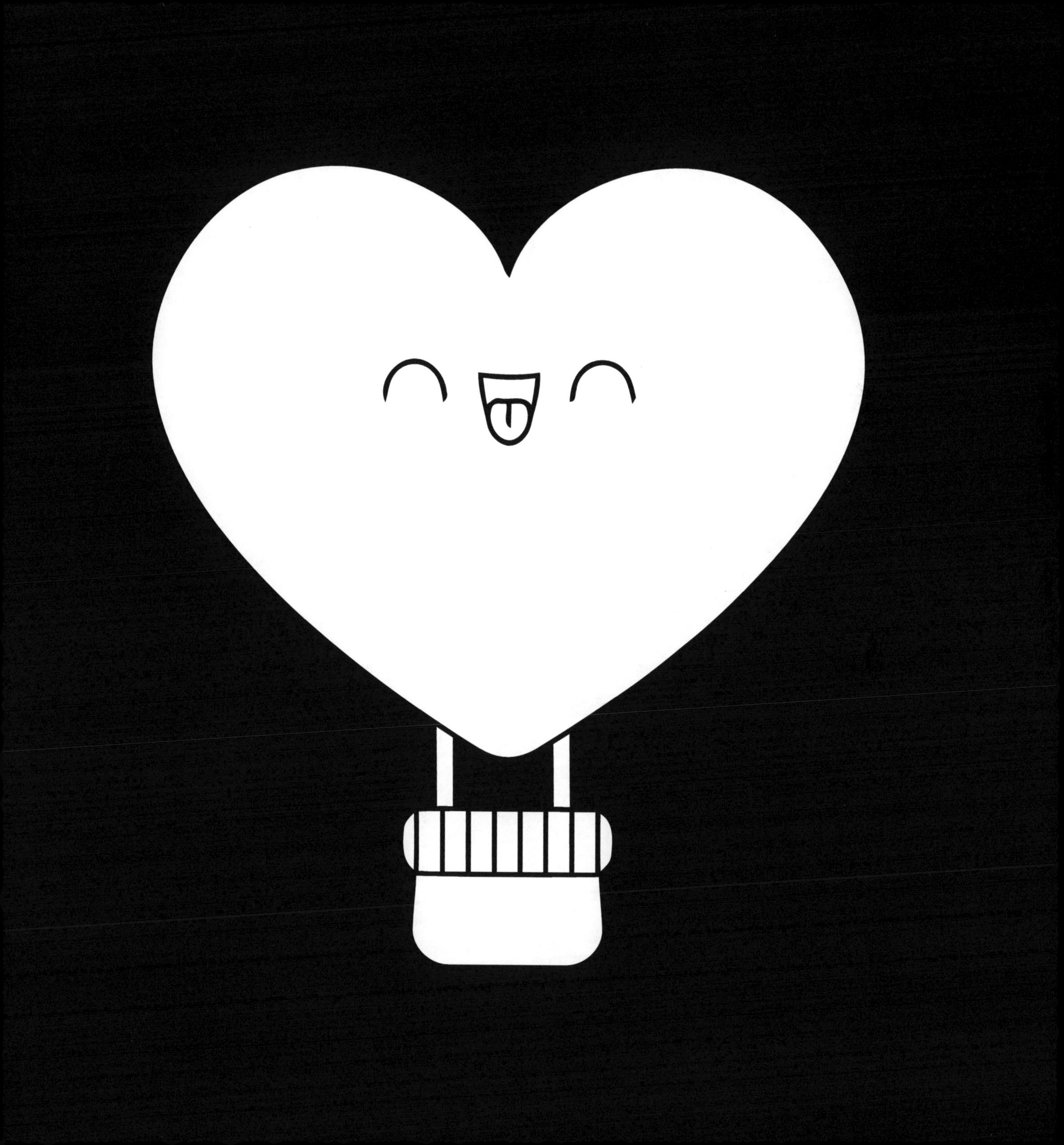

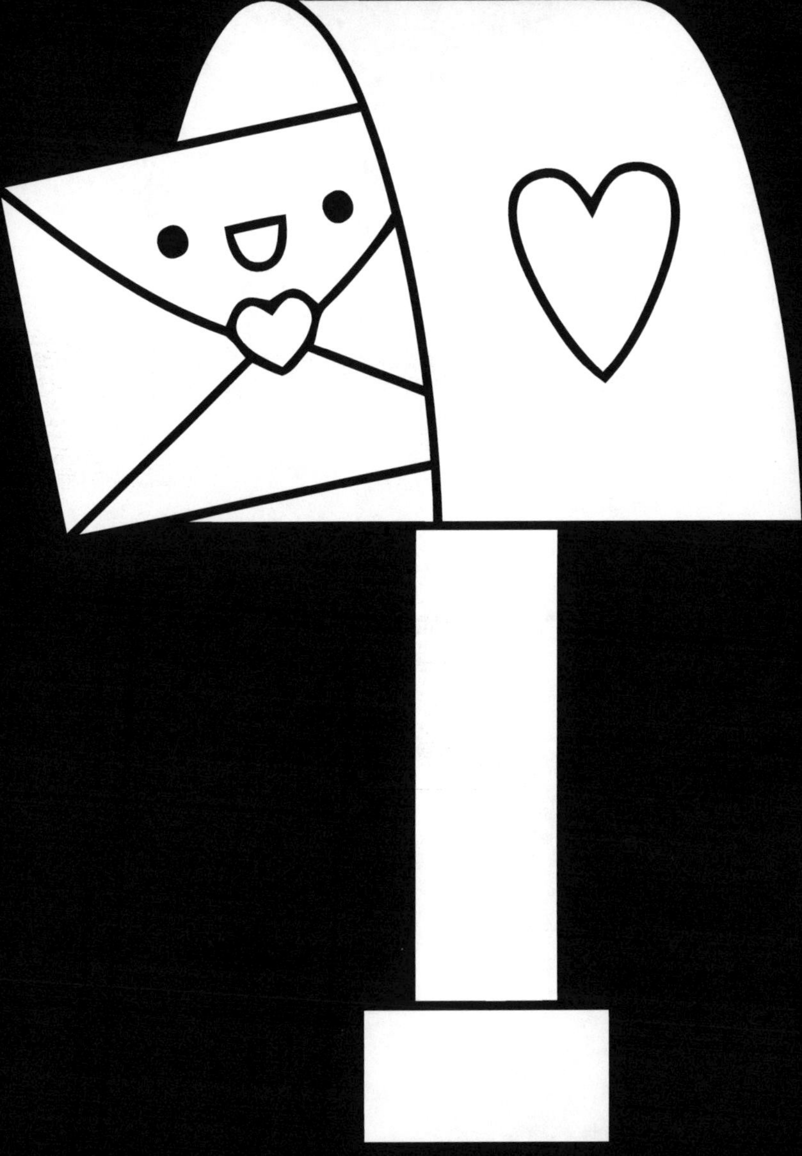

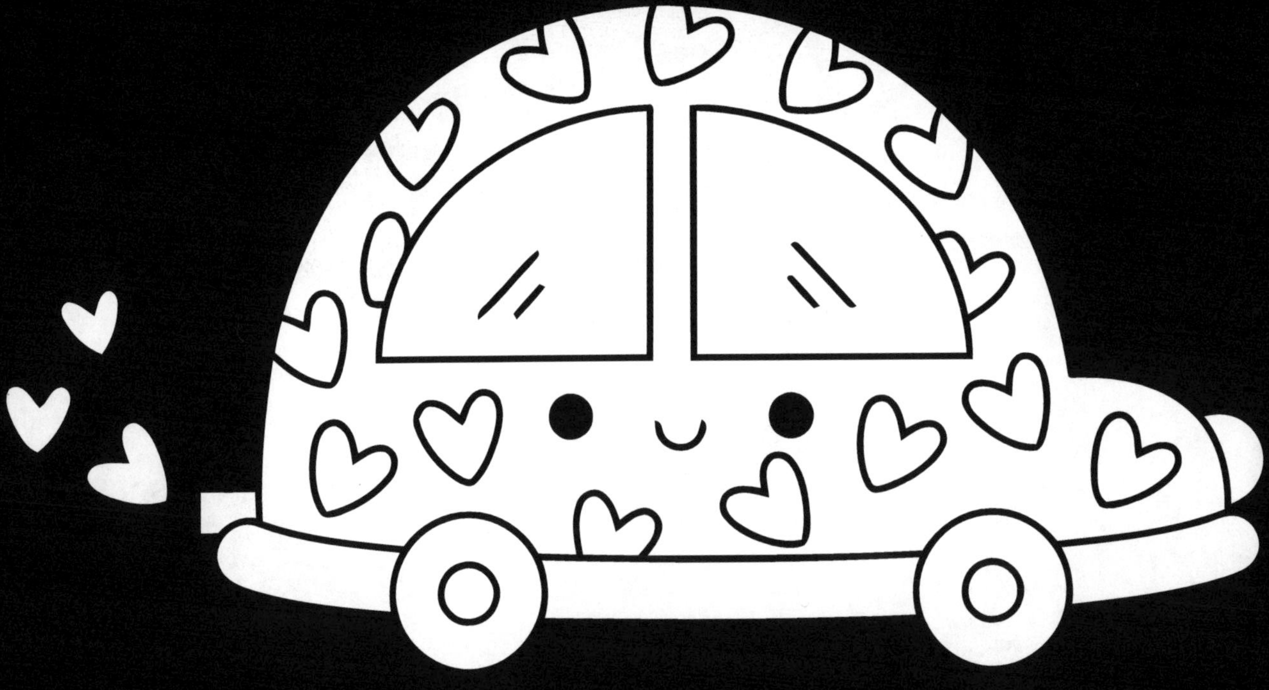

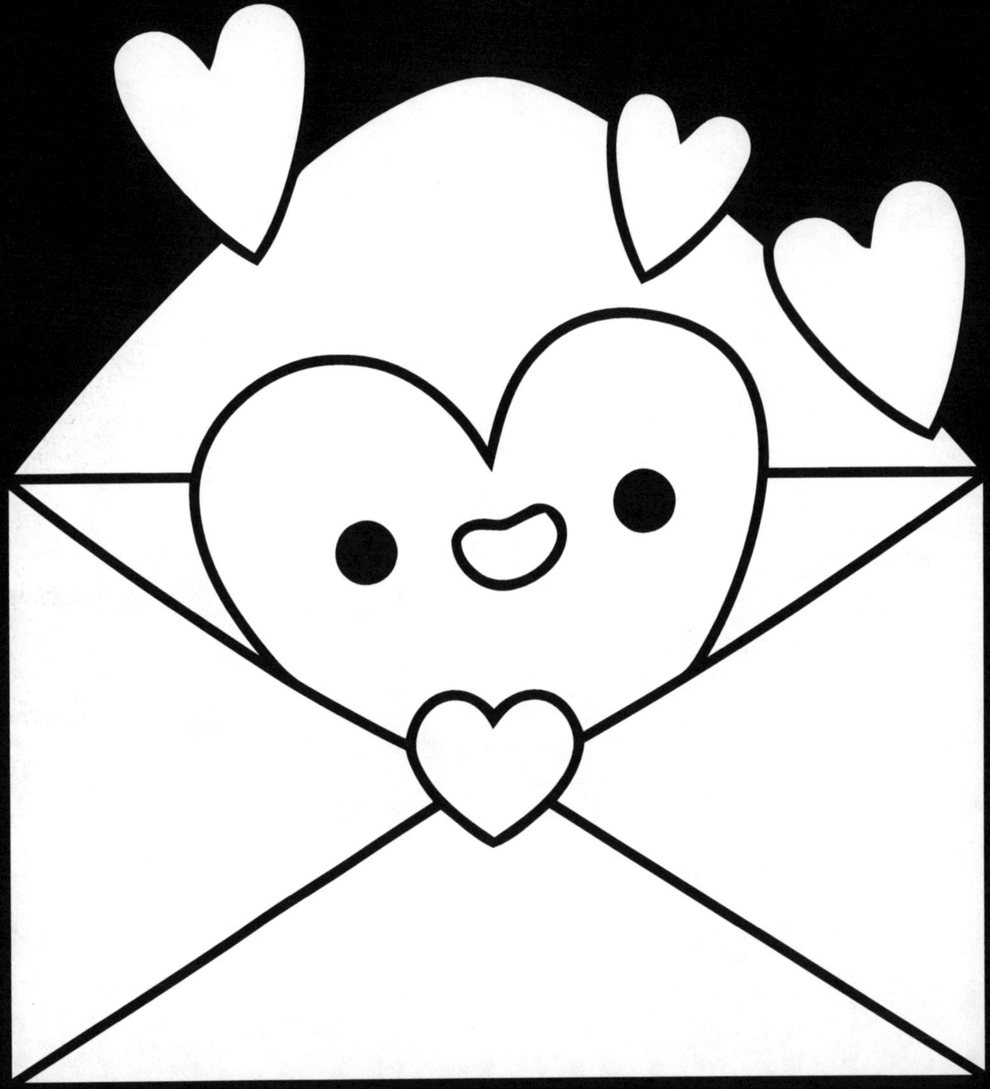

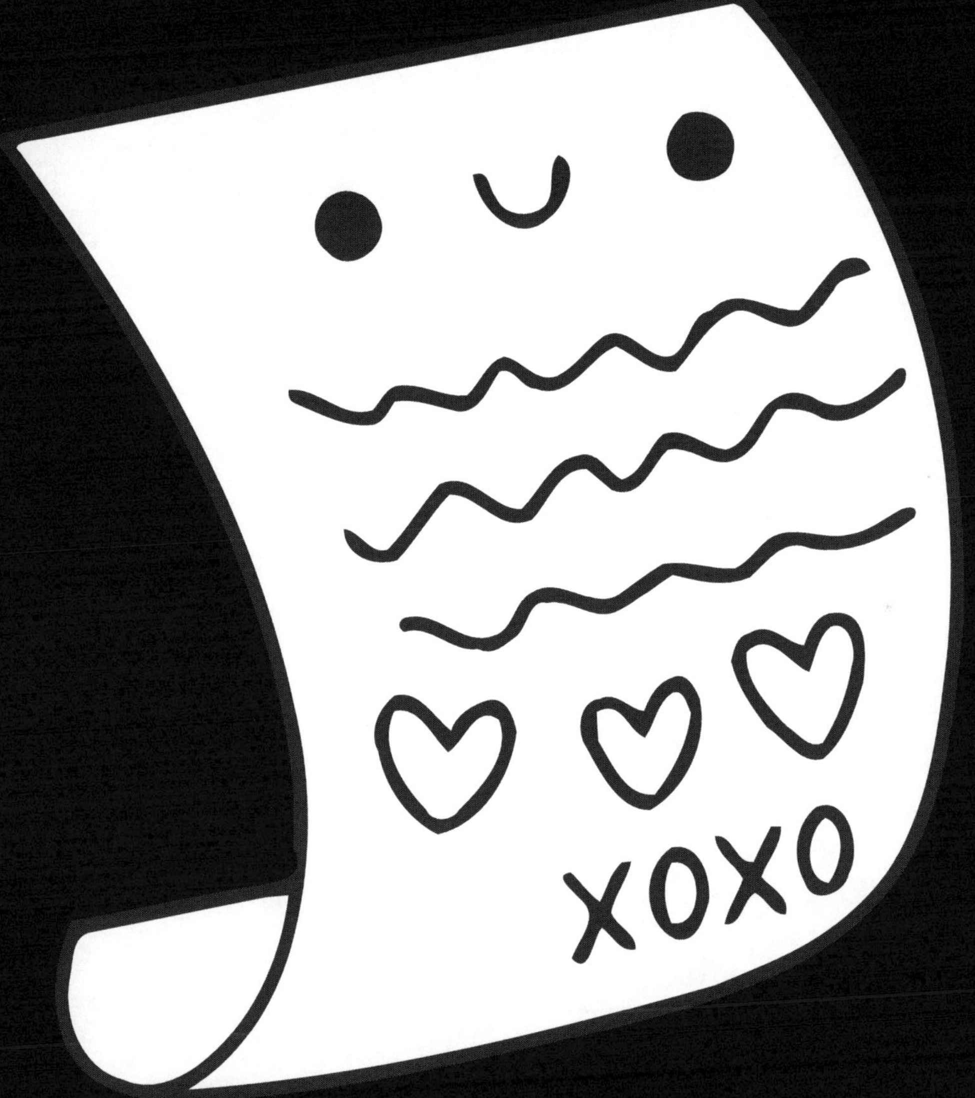
XOXO

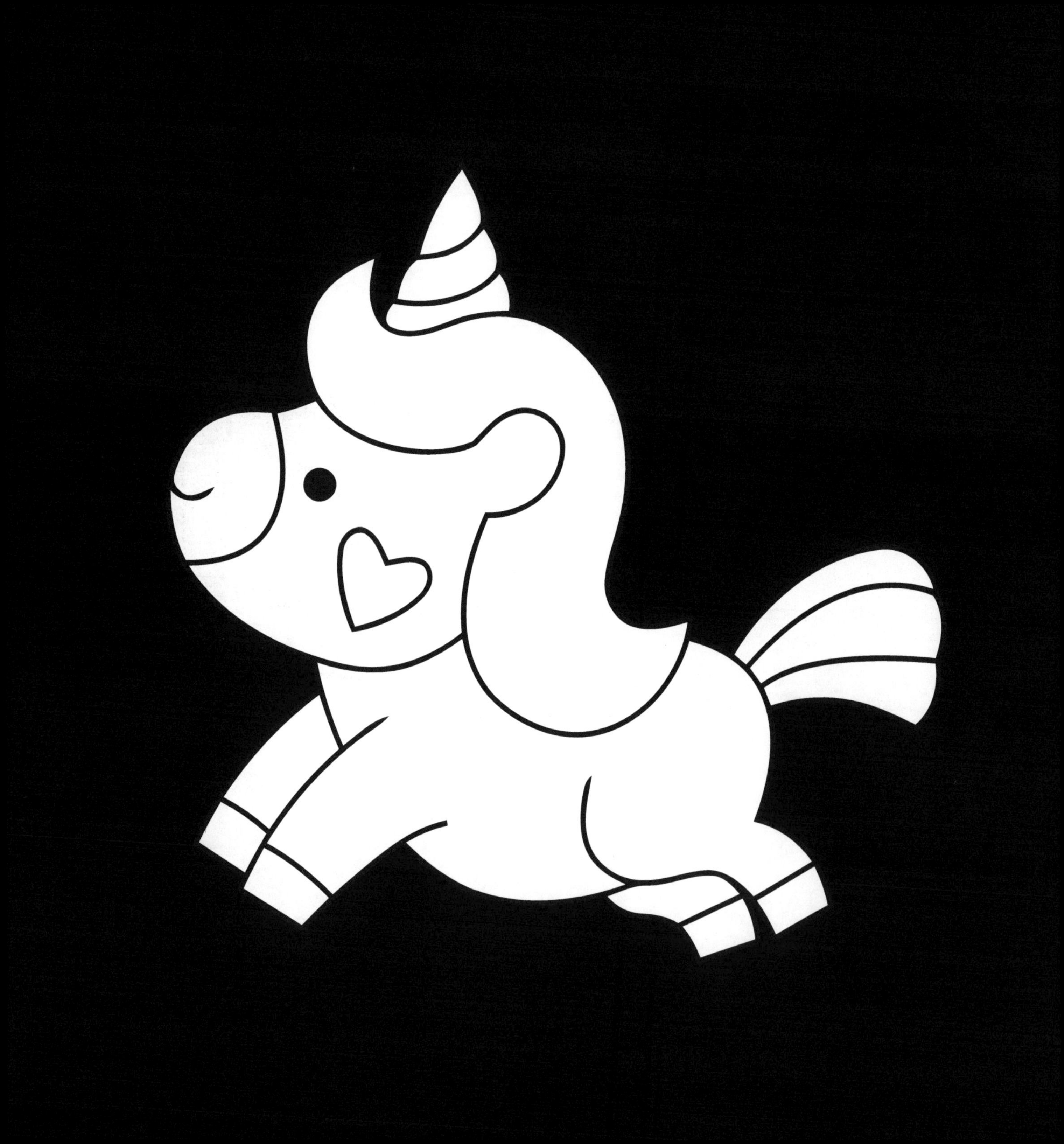

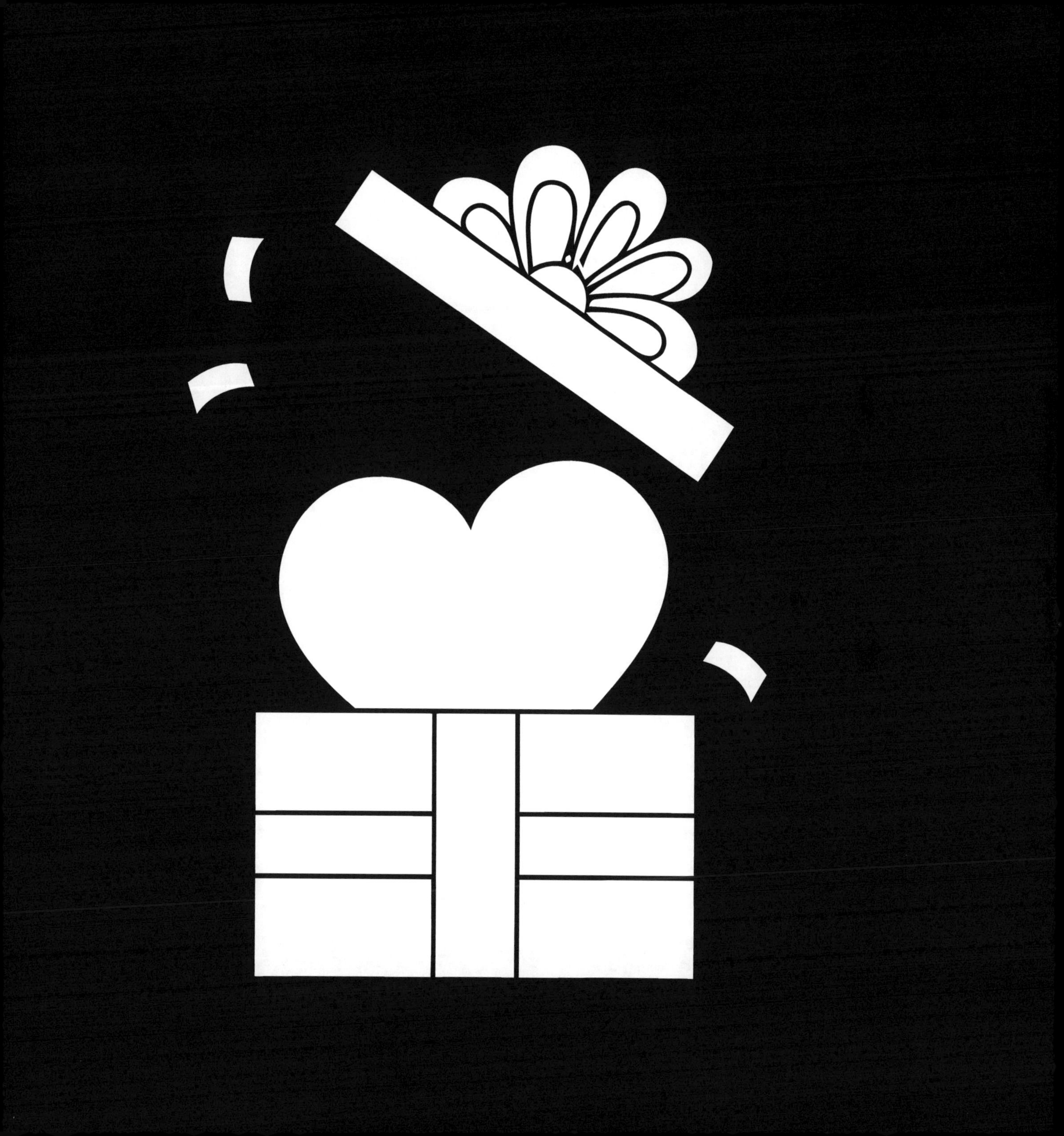

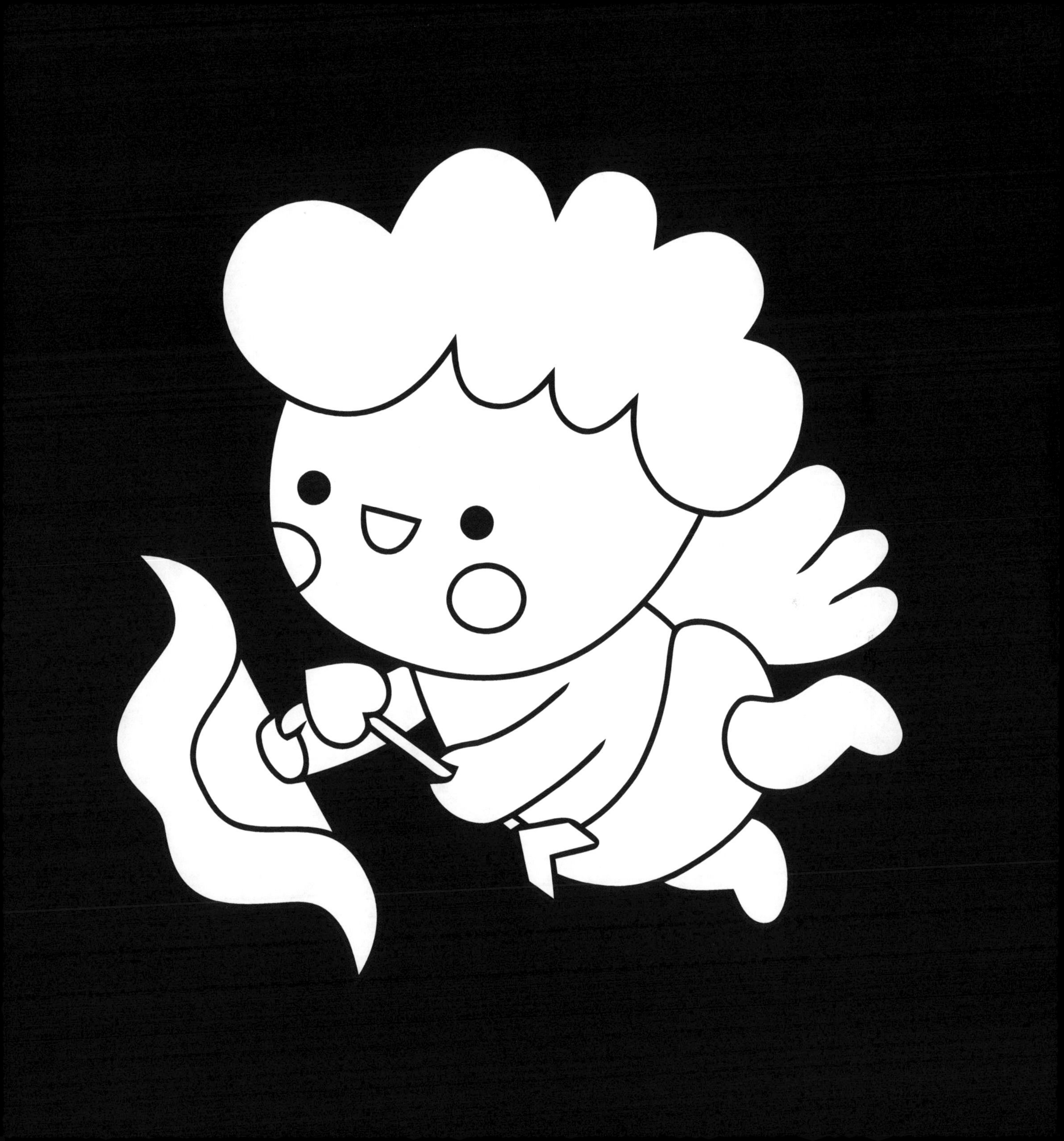

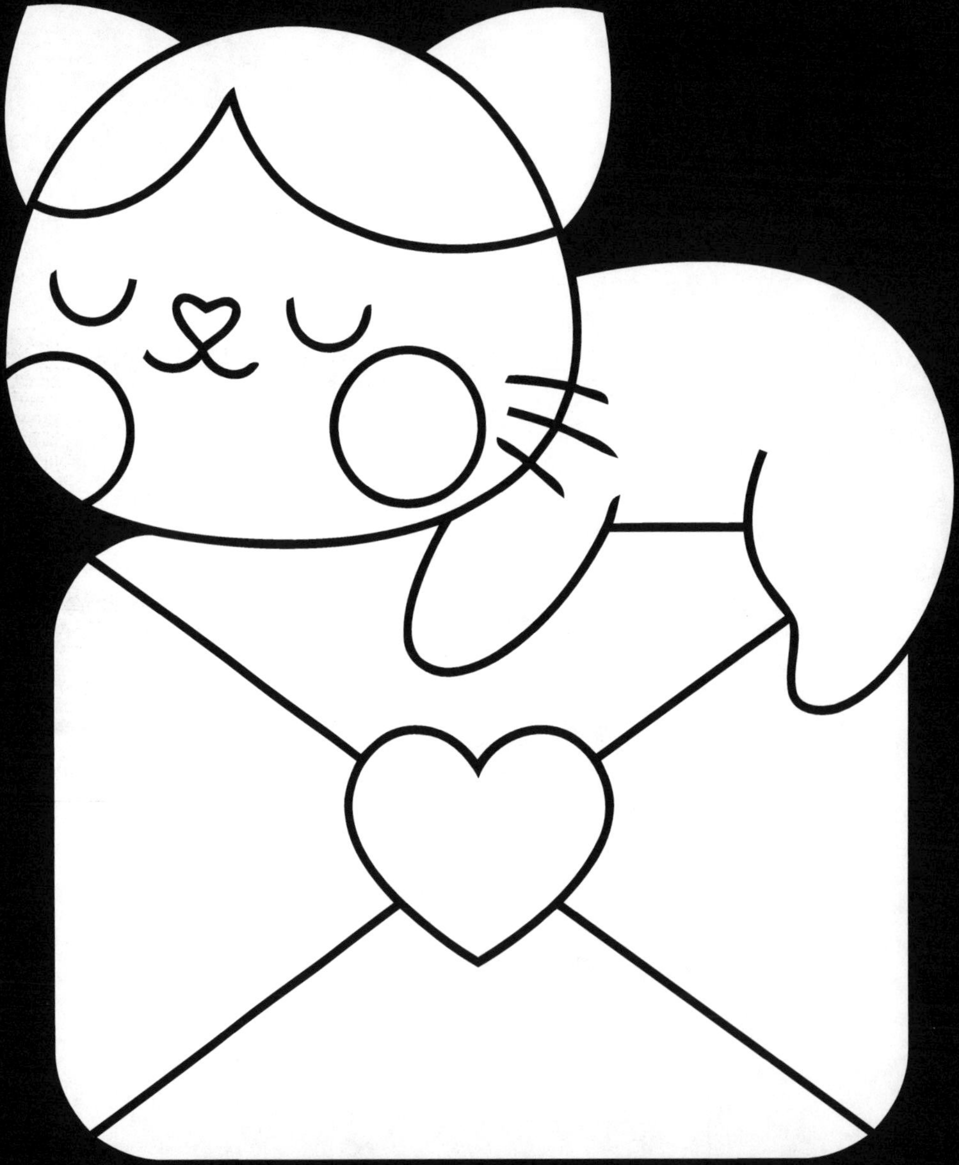

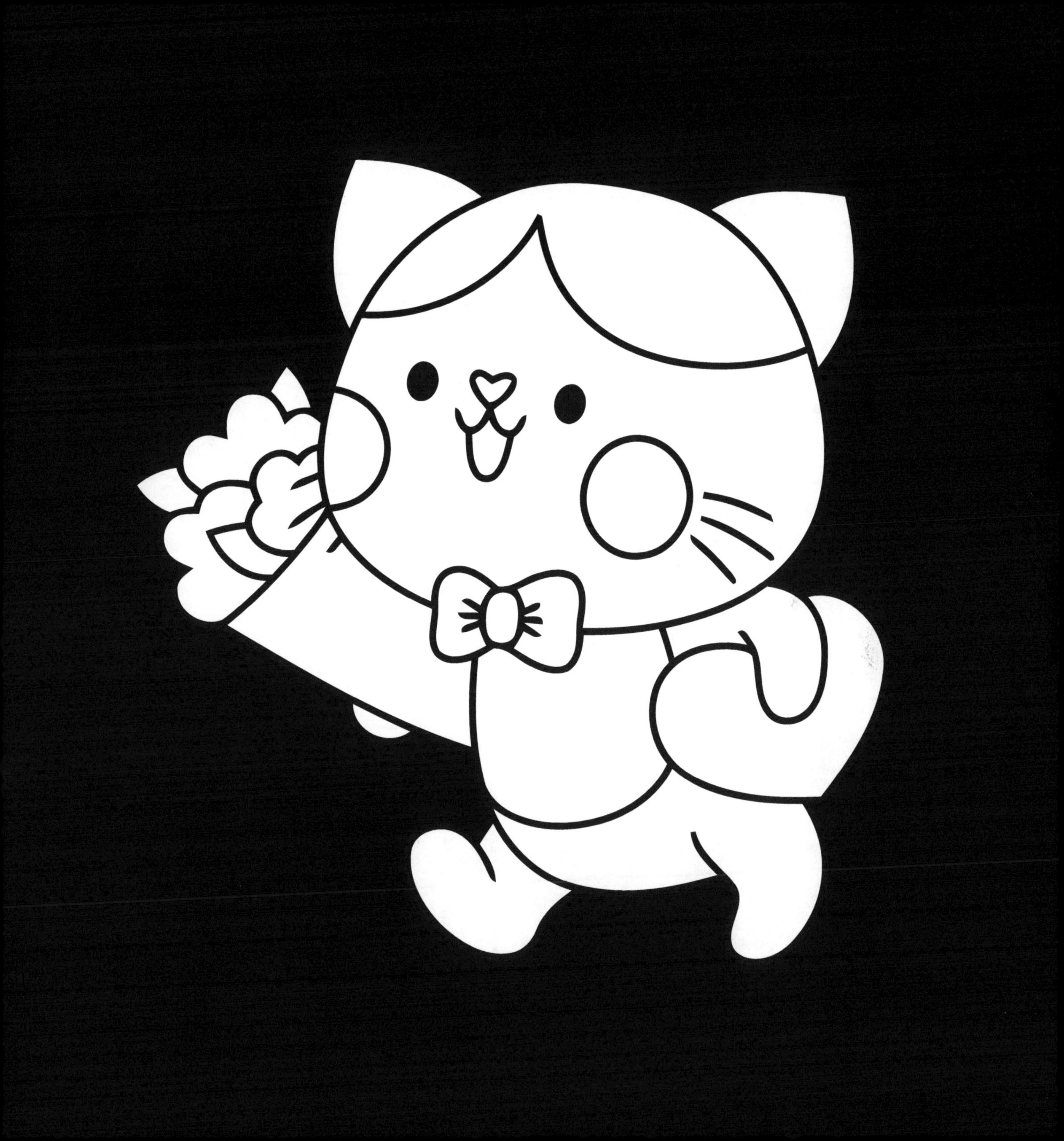

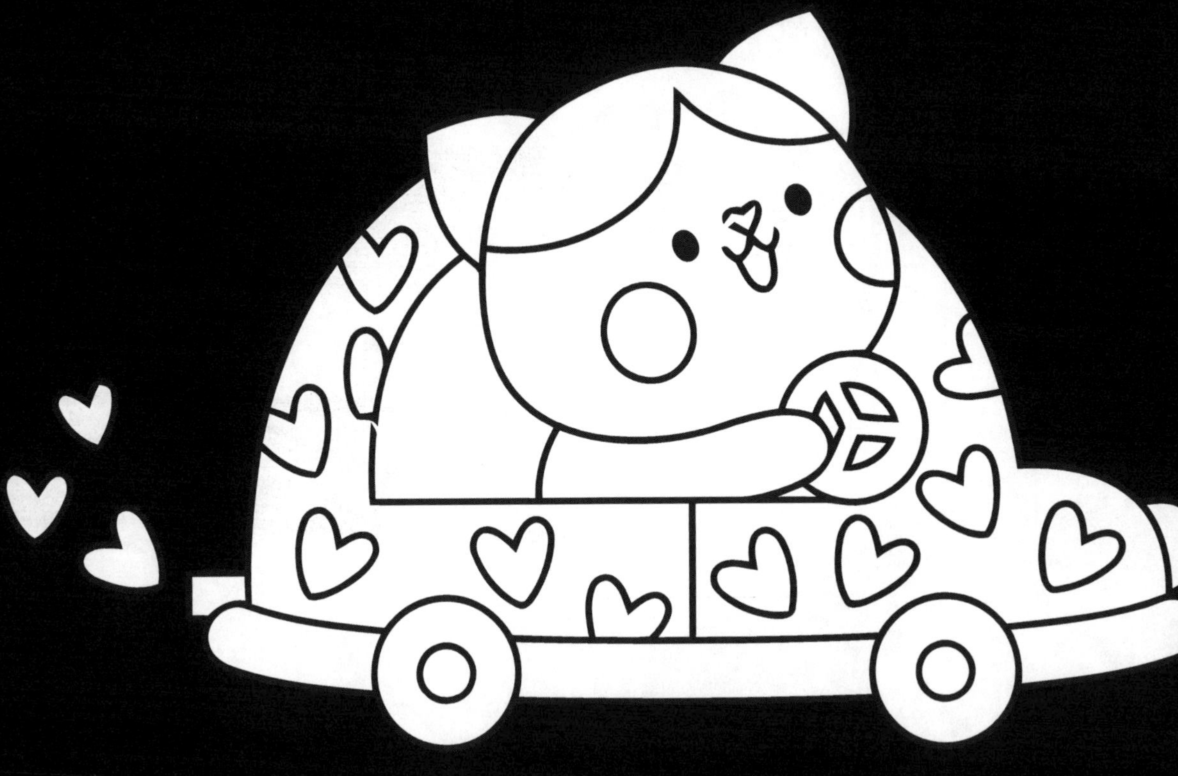

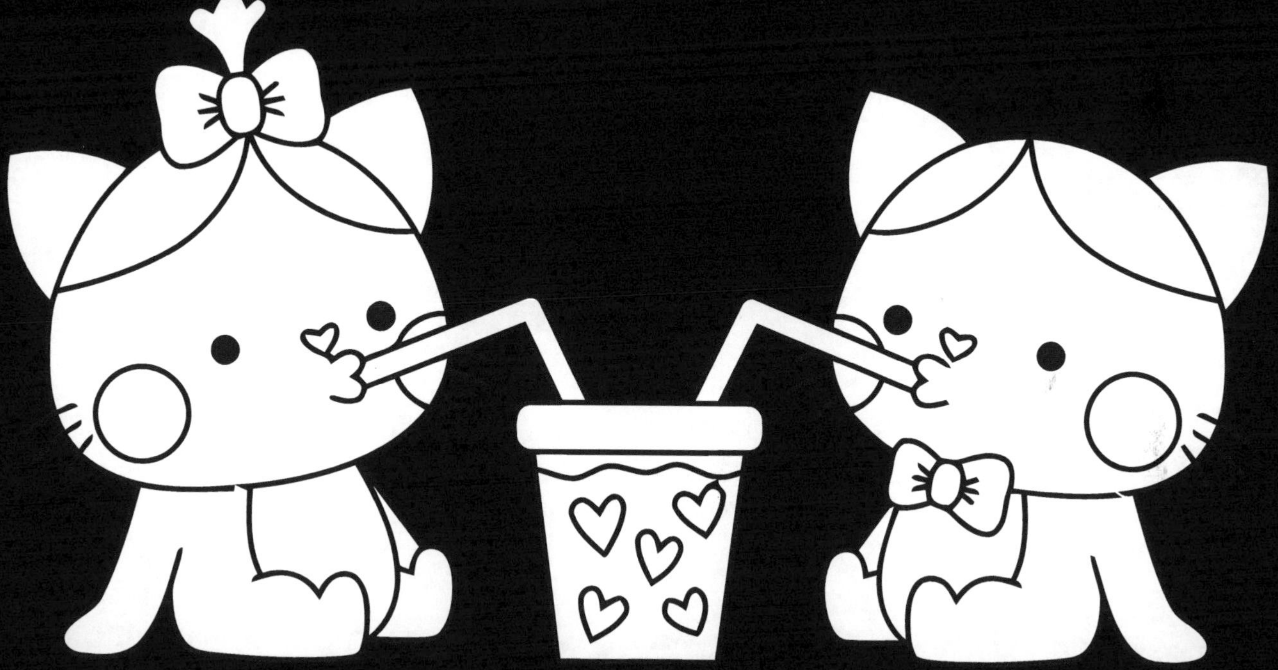

LOVE

Made in the USA
Middletown, DE
31 January 2024

48847349R00027